THE SCIENCE OF GETTING RICH

HOW TO THINK, HOW TO ACT, & WHAT TO DO TO HARNESS YOUR CREATIVE POTENTIAL

BY WALLACE D. WATTLES
WITH RYAN J. RHOADES

The Science of Getting Rich:
How to Think, How to Act, & What to Do to Harness Your Creative Potential

by Wallace Wattles with Ryan J. Rhoades

© 2018 Reformation Designs, LLC All rights reserved. No part of this publication may be reproduced, stored in a retrieval system or transmitted in any form or by any means, electronic, mechanical, photocopying, recording or otherwise without the prior permission of the publisher or in accordance with the provisions of the Copyright, Designs and Patents Act 1988 or under the terms of any licence permitting limited copying issued by the Copyright Licensing Agency.

This book is for informational purposes only and is not intended to provide legal, accounting, medical, or other professional services. If you require legal advice or other expert assistance, make sure to seek the services of a professional. Also, we disclaim any liability from actions you may take after reading this book and do not claim to be special gurus or anything of that sort. In a nutshell, we make no guarantees as to any particular financial results that you may or may not see from reading this.

The publisher has made every effort to ensure accurate information, web addresses, and contact information at the time of publishing. However, we assume no responsibility for errors or changes that occur after publication. If you do find errors, please contact us at www.ReformDesigns.biz and we will do our best to update the book for future editions.

Original publication by Wallace Wattles is in the public domain. Some pronouns and minor content edits have been made to make communication clearer to a modern audience.

Published, Cover Art, Commentary & Interior Design by Ryan J. Rhoades & Reformation Designs, LLC

ISBN-10: 1541209249

ISBN-13: 978-1541209244

Distributed by:
Reformation Designs, LLC
Salem, Oregon
www.ReformDesigns.biz

ACKNOWLEDGEMENTS

You are the reason that I create.

My team and I could not do what we do without the love and support of countless people from all around the world.

If you are reading this right now, you are one of those people.

You have helped us build a life around what we love and the pursuit of our ideas, our art, and our creativity. For that, we cannot thank you enough.

Your value and self-worth is not defined by the numbers in your bank account, how much or how hard you work or how many shares of stock you hold.

You have within you the power to bring creative solutions to all kinds of problems, big and small.

It is my hope that this book helps you along that path.

It has done so for me.

This is for you, your family, your friends, and your tribe.

Thanks for joining us on this journey so far.

May abundance, peace, joy, love, hope, creativity, and inspiration be yours all the days of your life.

ENDORSEMENTS

"Ryan & Laura at Reformation Designs are two of the most driven, inspired, & creative people that I have come across. Their keen eye for sharp design and strong desire to always learn and better their craft makes them a team that I would recommend in a heartbeat. Check them out - you won't be disappointed."

- *Rick Frishman,* *best-selling author, publisher & founder of Author 101 University*

"Superheroes Ryan & Laura of Reformation Designs are awesome! They will engage & inspire your audience with their creative superpowers."

- *Jim Kwik,* *celebrity memory coach, business strategist, international speaker & founder at Kwik Learning & SuperheroYou*

"Ryan is very talented in creating living online communities that learn, act and fellowship. He has managed to connect people from around the world and unite them around common values. He is very skilled in inspiring others to learn a topic for themselves and to put that knowledge into practice by leading with example. He is a talented art director with an eye for details and harmony. He thinks outside boxes. He inspires others to do likewise.

He is bold but humble. He genuinely cares for others and has a heart towards helping others reaching their potential. As a video producer he is extremely skilled, both in filming, scripting, lighting, knowing how to perform in front of a camera and last but not least post production, where his skills really comes into light."

- *Christoffer Björkskog ,* *Head of Development at Genero Digital Agency*

ENDORSEMENTS

"Ryan is the type of professional we all long for. High quality work, prompt in his response *(phone calls no less)*, and nothing but a pleasure to work with. I've almost lost all the hair on my head sending copious notes of errors to developers who were supposed to be fixing things. Reformation Designs produces first rate work AND is reliable - a combination which is SO hard to find."

- **Shana Dressler,** *Producer: The Future of Work - AIGA/NY & Former Executive Director of Google's 30 Weeks Design/Tech Incubator*

"Ryan is one of the most creative minds I know of. He is a man full of impeccable integrity and excellent interpersonal skills. If you need an über-skilled designer, brilliant help fleshing out your ideas, or if you have a message to share with world and need to give it wings, he's your man. I give him my highest recommendation."

- **Mark Paulson,** *Java Developer at Alpha & Omega Semiconductor*

"Ryan came into our business, made our customers feel very comfortable, got them speaking about their experience in an authentic way, ultimately producing an engaging video for our website to introduce our gym. He's extremely creative and grounded in the reality that it's about a clear message first and foremost - and the creative flare makes it more interesting - but he's not like many artists who don't understand that the art can't be distracting from your message.

If you own a business that wants to build some effective content for attracting new leads, talk to this man! Highly recommended."

- **Yusuf Clack ,** *Owner & Fitness Instructor at ClackFit.com*

ENDORSEMENTS

"Ryan and Laura are a power team! They have a rare talent that allows them to take a complex idea and express it artistically in a simple way so that the average person can understand it in the blink of an eye. When you work with them, you can rest assured that your business and best interests are in good hands! I recommend Reformation Designs for anyone that wants to increase brand awareness."

- ***Maria Brophy,*** *author of "Art, Money & Success" and art licensing expert*

"There are an overwhelming number of ways to build a genuine audience and customer base. Working with Reformation Designs has consistently helped me discard the noise and distill down the truly helpful information that's unique to my platform. Their ability to see the individual and business model from a 360 degree view, and guide them on the path of least resistance is at the same time exciting, and comforting. They take out the confusion and distraction, leaving you with clear and achievable steps. Brilliant."

- ***Leslie Calderoni,*** *speaker & author at LeslieCalderoni.com*

"Ryan is a great example of one who keeps up with the important and relevant breakthroughs while side stepping the social quagmires that stall out so many other creative types. He has my highest recommendation to anyone looking for design, graphic, video, business, or marketing consultation/creation. His no-nonsense approach to business and commitment to simplicity and clarity in communication place him above and beyond in the class of creative professionals."

- ***Thomas Dover,*** *Founder at WiseFire Cafe*

ENDORSEMENTS

"While a lot of marketing firms are trying to make a sale that benefits them only, Ryan is obsessed with making his clients look amazing and stand out from the crowd. He is a freaking genius.

His out-of-the-box thinking, natural enthusiasm, and expertise in media strategies are among the many assets he brings to every client relationship. Whether he's doing custom video clips, logo design, or website rebranding, he keeps your end goals in sight.

If you want your company to stand out, talk to Ryan. His work and his integrity are top notch!"

*- **Jennifer Hofmann**, writer at JenniferHofmann.com*

"Ryan's graphics are among the top shared posts on our social media & are really getting Jack Canfield's name out there. The images were beautiful! We were spending a bunch of time putting together our own graphics in Photoshop but they didn't even compare to the work that Reformation Designs did. We will definitely use your services next time we need more of these beautiful graphics."

*- **Lexi Wagner**, marketing team leader at JackCanfield.com*

"Ryan has strong interpersonal and leadership skills and knows how to cast a vision and follow through and implement great design. He has strong technical design skills and is very customer service oriented."

*- **Ben Chu**, former finance lead at Google*

ENDORSEMENTS

"Ryan is one of the few leaders I know whose core values cause him to push others towards innovation. He has the ability not only to lay a solid vision for those around, but also to help others meet their own potential while navigating that vision. He is an empowering leader that, rather than giving easy answers, asks tough questions to get people to think. In this way, he enables others to become skilled in the art of critical thinking.

He is a flexible leader who knows how to roll with the punches. Perfection isn't his aim. He has consistently reminded those of us that have worked with him that making a mistake is an important part of the growth process that we inevitably have to go through if we want to see significant gains. I have had the privilege on more than one occasion to see Ryan train people. It is an inspiring process. He takes a lot of time to communicate ideas and give practical advice. If he does not know something, he often knows WHERE or HOW to get what he needs. His skill at networking is nothing short of mind blowing.

Most importantly, one of the abilities that I have seen him employ over and over again is the tenacity to take risks...to do hard things. If you set a challenge up before Ryan, he will not back down on it. He will find an inventive way to tackle the problem at hand.

As someone who has worked for and with Ryan, I have the utmost respect for his work ethic and integrity. I cannot say this enough: there are few leaders that know how to invest in those they lead. Ryan does this very well. He knows how to help people unlock their own potential in the most personal of ways.

- ***Cordell Winrow***, *fitness trainer and consultant*

NOTE FROM THE PUBLISHER

If you grew up in any kind of organized religion or church system like I did, I can pretty much guarantee that there will be certain phrases or ideas in this book that may make you uncomfortable or question if it's just "another one of those prosperity gospel, name-it and claim-it books".

Either that, or you're incredibly skeptical of anything that you might find labeled as "self-help". Maybe both.

I certainly struggled with a lot of that at first, but I was also fascinated by how the author talked about the creative process and how to go about harnessing it in a way that CREATED wealth instead of looking for ways to EARN it. When I first came across the original version of this book a number of years ago, I was also incredibly desperate to make something happen financially just to keep food on the table.

As a designer of various different types of media and a longtime writer, I have always been intrigued by creativity in general - and I found that this book helped give me more of an understanding of that process.

I believe, as does the original author of this book, that a huge part of tapping into the creative process starts with first visualizing the goals you want to achieve, writing down what you imagine, and - most importantly - **taking action to bring it to life.**

As you read, you will see this theme repeatedly mentioned in a variety of ways. I find that it is through regular repetition and discipline that we grow to be better at anything we do. *(This isn't rocket science of course, but how much of that realization do we regularly apply to our lives and business endeavors?)*

Often times the hardest part can be just getting started. We must learn to rest in the moment and create like when we were younger and less cynical about the world around us.

This is largely about using your imagination on purpose. Now that you're all grown up with a fancy job, property taxes and medical insurance or maybe some important sounding letters after your name, you very well may have forgotten how to access that childlike imagination.

I would like to propose to you that this quite possibly may be the reason that you're feeling stuck and frustrated with your life or business. *(I assume you are feeling that way at some level, otherwise you probably wouldn't be reading this book!)*

My goal - and the original author's goal, I believe - is to help you tap into your imagination again in order to solve your problems creatively and in a way that generates sustainable income for you and your family.

Don't misunderstand as you go through it - he is in no way *(as far as I can tell)* insinuating that you should simply sit around daydreaming.

Of course not! Nothing would ever get done.

He is saying that your imagination plays a huge part in the creative process, but that you should **spend your energy focusing on the things you can change and the things you can do rather than all of the things you can't.**

You'll see a lot of encouragement to **always do what you can, with what you have, where you are.** A vast majority of the "success" that we have had in our lives and business endeavors hinges solely on this concept.

If you grew up in church, the concept of "stewardship" should sound familiar to you. I believe a lot of what the author references throughout the book is speaking along those lines.

For example, you may not have a grand piano and want to learn how to play the piano. You may love the feeling of the weighted keys, and the amazing sound produced by a grand piano, but you also may not have the room for one, let alone the finances to afford it.

What you **can** do, however, is download any number of free or inexpensive software programs or apps on your phone, tablet or computer and learn how to play on a digital version in the interim.

You could also *(as I did)* keep an eye open at different thrift shops around your city; quite frequently you will find used or even new musical instruments for very cheap.

Additionally, there are often people giving away and selling musical instruments used or lightly used in local online marketplaces like Craigslist, Facebook, etc.

I taught myself how to play the piano with a keyboard that normally was $150+ that I found for $30 in great condition at a local thrift store. It even lights up when I play it!

It's taken a few years, but am now at a point where I am shopping around for a much higher quality instrument that I will know how to use much better because I worked with what I had available instead of the constant pursuit of *more*. (We also can struggle with wanting something perfect before we are willing/ready to get started. You'll never *feel* ready. Just get going!)

A huge part of all of this is learning to recognize and seize opportunities that others frequently overlook or miss.

If you decide to try this out, don't be surprised if other people start noticing and think of you as they come across instruments that someone is giving away or selling for cheap, especially as you grow in your skills and continue practicing some new art form.

I know a number of people that this has happened to just in my own immediate family, but it certainly doesn't happen overnight!

That said, **I do not claim to believe or adhere to every principle or idea that the author presents in this book.**

There are a number of things that I simply don't agree with for any number of reasons, and I am quite sure that you will find the same to be true for you. "Eat the meat and spit out the bones" and you'll do just fine.

There are also a number of things that I have found to be quite true in practice and with large amounts of testing over time. That is what "science" boils down to, anyway, right?

My goal in republishing this is not for the sake of trying to tell you what to think or believe.

I have wasted a lot of time doing that over the years and have found that life is an ever-changing and ever-evolving dance of ideas, concepts, beliefs, successes, failures, and pursuits.

I try my hardest not to be nearly as dogmatic as I used to be about a whole lot of different things. It gets too stressful trying to fulfill the insatiable and unattainable goal of trying to be right all the time.

I don't claim for one second to be the authority on "getting rich" - at least not simply in a financial sense or how much money I have in my bank account as compared to a whole lot of other people on this floating blue rock we call Earth.

At the time of this writing, I have just as many concerns about cash-flow as you do, and maybe even more, but I also know a lot of people who have bigger concerns because their bills have more zeroes at the end of them.

Additionally, I know that **it is oftentimes the perspective we choose to take that determines how well or how quickly we solve a problem.**

This book has been one of a number of books I've read that has helped me realize the riches that I do have (food, water, shelter, family, friends, freedom to create). It has helped me learn how to focus on being thankful for what I have, rather than constantly seeking more just for the sake of having more.

(For additional reading recommendations on this topic and more, check out the back of the book in the appendix.)

"Being rich," as far as I see it anyway, isn't about the constant pursuit of more material or cash-based wealth as much as it is about being content with what you have, which will always lead to more expansion.

If you gave Leonardo Da Vinci a crappy paintbrush, chances are he'd still paint a pretty darn good piece of art even without the most expensive brushes on the market.

It's not about the tools, it's about the artist and the time and attention spent learning the ins and outs of the craft.

Sure, everyone wants to have the best tools available - but I have found over the years that if I get stuck on that, I don't create.

If I focus on being thankful for what I **do** have and what I **can** use, I am easily able to shift into "the zone" and start making the things I have set out to make.

For me, *The Science of Getting Rich* isn't so much THE absolute "how-to" manual *(as the author states or heavily implies a few times)* - but it certainly is **A** how-to manual in a vast sea of others that can help you along your journey of creative discovery.

My hope is that you will find a number of the perspectives presented in this short book are very helpful for understanding how to unlock and harness the creative process.

I go back and reread it regularly and hope that you will as well.

(Just a heads up, if you are familiar with the original text, you may notice that some of the language and pronouns have been updated or edited slightly to make communicating the core message of the book simpler for today's audience.

*You will also notice I have added my own commentary at certain points; you'll see my initials **RJR** prior to any commentary.)*

I wish you abundance, joy, wisdom, more creative ideas than you know what to do with, and the freedom to explore all that which makes you come alive.

Here's to you and your pursuit of making the world a better place through your creativity!

Enjoy - and go create something amazing!

INTRODUCTION BY RYAN J. RHOADES

"FORMLESS SUBSTANCE," FOCUS, & IMAGINATION:
How to Make Something from Nothing

"When you grow up, you tend to get told the world is the way it is and your life is just to live your life inside the world. Try not to bash into the walls too much. Try to have a nice family, have fun, save a little money. That's a very limited life.

Life can be much broader once you discover one simple fact: Everything around you that you call life was made up by people that were no smarter than you.

You can change it, you can influence it, you can build your own things that other people can use.

Once you learn that, you'll never be the same again."

— *Steve Jobs (1955 - 2011)*

Your realization of the concept in the quote above can truly change your life. I don't say that to be dramatic. I say it because I know that it has changed mine. It is my hope that this book will help you redirect your life in a positive way, as I know that it has helped me to do the same.

It has taken me years and years of practice, struggle, more practice, frustration, almost insane amounts of reading and research, and lots and lots of trial and error, but the fact that you are holding this book in your hand right now is proof of this concept.

As a longtime writer, designer and multimedia producer, one of the things that I have always been fascinated by is the ability for people to envision something in their minds and then, through some sort of mental, physical, or technological sorcery, create the very thing that they had imagined.

Our minds are powerful instruments indeed, and if you can learn to harness yours and tune out *(or at the very least turn down)* the noise and chatter that can so often fill it, you too will start to experience the never-ending excitement that can come with the act of leaning into your own creativity.

That is just one of the things you will begin to experience and understand how to harness as you read through this simple but powerful book. But before we get into all of that, I first would like to share a bit of background to lay the foundation for what you're about to read.

When I was a kid, I spent a lot of time in my aunt and uncle's print shop. In the late 1980's and early 1990's, computers were just starting to show up in people's homes, and they had started their own printing business.

They had some of the first computers I had ever seen and it never ceased to amaze me to watch something that once only existed within the screen come to life when sent to the printing press.

My mother was a public school teacher, so we eventually got access to one of the early Macintosh computers. I remember one of the first things I did was look for ways to draw digital pictures on a blank digital canvas.

There was a particular painting program *(similar to Microsoft Paint on Windows computers)* that got my attention.

One of my first digital creations was a fake movie poster depicting some terrified earthworms fleeing from a giant beak fishing around in the soil.

There were no colors in the monitor, so everything we did at that time was in black and white.

I drew ragged-looking, giant block letters with the mouse and wrote the title of my imaginary movie: *"BEAK"* — and I was hooked.

I printed it out and was fascinated by the fact that I had just done some sort of digital wizardry and now was holding something that had once only existed in my imagination.

And of course there were sequels.

"BEAK II: Revenge," "BEAK Returns," and countless more. As time went on and the technology improved, we were introduced to color screens.

Each installment of these digital creations got more and more detailed, with more earthworms meeting their untimely demise in the mouth of this imaginary digital bird that was never fully revealed *(primarily because anytime I tried drawing a whole bird it looked so ridiculous that I couldn't bring myself to show it to anyone).*

Eventually, we started using some greeting card production programs; I remember one of them was called Print Shop Pro. We would design and print out our own greeting cards and give them to family members for holidays, birthdays, etc.

I also would occasionally write short stories, print them out and staple them together, making my own little books.

I spent a lot of time tinkering around with the software, looking for any way that I could to take what I was imagining and turn it into something tangible. I made buttons, signs, magnets, t-shirts...all kinds of things. Every time I made something new, I would find ways to make it better the next time.

I was very fortunate to have parents who cultivated and encouraged this kind of creative pursuit in me. I was always given the freedom to draw, or build, or play with toys that would give me some kind of blank canvas to work with like LEGO's, the Etch-a-Sketch, or Lincoln Logs.

If you are a parent, I can't recommend enough that you constantly encourage the creative pursuits of your children.

Music, art, writing, architecture, 3D design, filmmaking, dancing, painting… all forms of creative expression will help them better understand themselves and the world around them. It will empower them to learn to work with their imagination to create amazing products and experiences for themselves and others, for which they can later learn to charge a pretty penny.

If you couldn't tell from my BEAK story, I also grew up watching a lot of cheesy sci-fi and monster movies like Godzilla, Jason and the Argonauts, Gremlins, Jaws, etc.

In the same way that I was fascinated by the creations my aunt and uncle would make in their print shop and the things we were able to make with our Macintosh at home, it blew my mind that people could take clay, plaster, or other materials and create imaginary monsters for movie heroes to fight against.

This was well before the era of computer generated images (CGI), but still *I was hooked.*

My dad and I would often stay up late into the night watching the behind-the-scenes videos of how the movie magic happened.

I learned all about green screens, claymation, and puppets…and then watched a bunch of adults do a lot of fun things that I didn't often see anyone doing anywhere other than on the TV. It made me want to learn everything I could about movie makeup, special effects, and film.

Eventually, all I knew was that I wanted to figure out how I could make a living having fun and making fun ideas come to life.

The seed of that concept showed up early for me, but it is only now probably 25 years later that I am realizing how much of that time spent cultivating my creativity has led us to where we are now.

My team and I have worked with amazing people from all over the planet through the magic of the internet. The things that we are now able to create with computers, tablets, and smart phones, as well as additional technology that is available to so many people in our world today, is just mind blowing.

It is my hope that you start recognizing and capitalizing on this fact.

It is a truly amazing thing that some of the financially "poorest" people in the world, right this very moment, have access to information and abilities that even the kings and queens of the earth couldn't imagine just 50 years ago.

You can communicate with someone on the other side of the world instantaneously with a video call through Skype, Facetime, Facebook, Zoom, Google Hangouts, or any number of other countless programs. It's the closest thing to teleportation that we've currently got, people! That's awesome!

You can immediately find the answer to just about any question *(or at least start yourself on the right track)* at the speed of thought just by doing a few simple internet searches from your phone.

That is game-changing. A lot of people who have grown up with the world like this don't realize the power to create that is well within their grasp and quite literally at their fingertips. I aim to change that.

Looking back, all of these things have had a huge impact on my life and career choices. I still make my own products, creations, and designs come to life. I am blessed to be able to now do what I love and actually get paid well for it. It has taken a great deal of time and effort in order to be able to say that, and a big part of it is learning to recognize the value and worth that your creativity can bring to the marketplace.

For example, in our home, the majority of the coffee mugs that we have are our own designs. Most of the t-shirts and hooded sweatshirts that I wear are our own designs. The posters hung up in my office and a lot of the artwork around our apartment is our own work.

We don't do this to be narcissistic or self-congratulatory. **We do these things as a constant reminder that we really CAN create the world we want to live in and to surround ourselves with things that encourage us to always pursue what we love and the betterment of our craft.**

That brings me to why I'm publishing a new version of this book that you now hold in your hands *(or are reading on one of your devices)*.

I came across *The Science of Getting Rich* in a thrift store a number of years ago. At the time, I was struggling financially in some pretty intense ways. I didn't even know where my rent money was going to come from. Over the years, my wife and I have had a number of difficult struggles to overcome in our journey and oftentimes when I am feeling stuck, I go browsing old books in thrift shops or in my public library.

Upon initially glancing through this little book, I have to admit that I scoffed at a lot of it.

"How could there be a SCIENCE to getting RICH?" I wondered. Especially coming from a place where I had very little money in the bank at the time, I was even more skeptical.

Even still, the author seemed very insistent that his methods would work, and, well…I was desperate for something to get me out of the hole we were in. So, I spent a few dollars, brought it home and started reading it.

The language in it was hard to get through at times. There were plenty of instances where I struggled through it because it felt so ridiculous, especially when my bank account was draining, we weren't finding any new clients, and I didn't know how I was going to pay my bills.

…but something about it kept me reading.

Maybe it was the certainty with which the author wrote. Maybe it was the fact that I was at a place where I needed to make something happen so badly that I was willing to try anything. Whatever it was, I'm glad that I did. Once I finally started realizing that the author was mostly referring to the creative process when he talked about what he calls "The Certain Way," a bunch of things started clicking into place for me.

The creative process in general has always been something that has captivated my attention. A big part of my life's work *(and I believe my life's purpose)* is to help others harness their own creativity and bring it to full expression.

We have published books, created entire product lines *(which you can check out at RDShop.biz)*, built businesses, created marketing campaigns, hosted events, planned parties, raised money for charity, made copious amounts of flyers and business cards, built websites, released music albums *(soundcloud.com/ReformDesigns)*, held art shows, and countless other "creative" things - **but what they all have in common is that the first step is having an idea.**

The first step is dreaming up the concept.

It could start with just a fleeting thought flashing through the subconscious - whether in the form of a mental image or a word or a song playing somewhere in our mind doesn't matter. What matters is what you do with it.

The whole creative process starts like a seed.

Bringing ideas to life is easier when you think of them like seeds, and your canvas like soil.

The time and energy you spend tending to that soil *(working on your canvas)* acts like water and sunlight that causes that seed to grow.

Eventually, the seed will come to fruition and your ideas will come to life as you learn to better harness your creativity and your craft.

Throughout this book, you will see the author repeatedly refer to what he calls "formless substance."

It took me awhile to figure out what he was talking about, but over the years I have interpreted that phrase as any kind of blank canvas: physical, digital or otherwise.

A blank piece of paper.

An empty room.

A blinking cursor on an empty screen.

A lump of clay.

A new relationship.

A green screen.

A blank sheet of music.

A napkin in a restaurant.

You get the idea.

These things *(and many others that I'm sure you could now think of)* are all "formless substances" until acted upon by you and your imagination.

As you read, if you feel yourself getting confused, try to slow down and write down what you're stuck on or what is causing you to feel stuck, then keep reading and come back to the question later. You may find it is answered as you continue along. I know that was the case for me.

I would highly encourage note-taking as you go along. Maybe write some notes to yourself in a new notebook or in the margins *(or if you're reading this on a digital device, take some notes on that)*. I've also included pages for note taking at the end of the book in the appendix.

I am republishing this book *(which is in the public domain)* because I wanted to help breathe fresh life and a bit of my own commentary into something that has made a big difference in my creative and business pursuits over the years.

I have found that the philosophies and suggestions within it have enabled me to think more creatively and critically about problems that I am facing. Rather than looking to outside sources for help, it has helped me instead to begin looking inward and working to figure out creative ways to fix things or make something new.

Throughout you will find footnotes and other commentary that are my own thoughts and examples, all while keeping in mind our very digital and fast-paced age.

Creativity is not something that I ever encourage rushing, unless you are trying to simply get better at creating what you imagine faster for the sake of improving your own craft.

This book has helped me in a number of ways, not the least of which is the almost constant reminder to give myself the grace to embrace the creative process and trust that as long as I just keep working at something, eventually I'll see it come to life.

Spending a little bit of time on your creative or business pursuits every day is a great way to see major progress over time.

You may have picked this up because you were looking for a way to make money - and you certainly can use it that way - but for me, and I believe for Mr. Wattles as well, being rich isn't always (or even often) about how much money you have in the bank.

Being rich is about being content with what you have and learning how to find that contentment with what's right in front of you. It's about leaning into the process of creativity and tapping into the power that is within you to make something of value.

Being rich is being able to manifest the very things that you are wanting to create in order to make the world a better place than you found it.

I have found more than anything that this book has helped me figure out more practical ways to harness my own creativity and make something out of nothing.

There is nothing quite like holding something in your hands that once only existed in your imagination or on a digital screen.

I hope that this book and my commentary on it helps you in the realization of your goals and dreams. I have formatted it in a way that I hope is easy to digest and with plenty of room for you to take your own notes at the end.

I in no way claim perfection or that I am some special guru with special knowledge. What you choose to do with what you learn here is your decision alone.

We all have made mistakes and have regrets, but one thing I do know is that I have never regretted any time that I have spent cultivating my creativity or my ability to manifest the things I once could only imagine. I have never regretted any time I have spent reading books on subjects that interest me and that inspire me to be better today than I was yesterday.

I have read this book again and again - not always from cover to cover, but often times I will pick it up when I am feeling stuck, frustrated, or can't figure out the answer to a creative problem I am trying to solve.

In a number of ways, although it is a short book, I have found that it has often been a great resource to keep within reach as the advice in it has helped me more times than I can count.

I wish the same for you.

If you have never had anyone give you permission or encouragement to pursue your passion, live your dreams, paint that picture, take that course, learn that language, write that book, or play that instrument…let this be it.

Don't wait for some mystical sign. Learn to re-embrace the child-likeness and imagination required to fully excel in any creative or business pursuit. It takes time, but I assure you that it is worth it.

This book should help you not just with practical matters, but with spiritual, emotional, and mental matters as well.

It also has been very helpful for me in navigating the extreme uncertainty of the times in which we live, as I have recognized that the struggles that we all face in this life can often be overcome if we look to those who have gone before us for clues on how to proceed.

Tom-Butler-Bowdon says of Mr. Wattles' background:

> *"In 1890's and 1900's America, many people felt oppressed by a system where great industrial trusts and extremely wealthy individuals held sway. Bill Gates is often seen as the richest capitalist of our age, but in relative terms, he did not match the wealth of Rockefeller and Carnegie in their time.*
>
> *In a more brutal economic era without safety nets, the average person clung onto jobs they hated or kept up businesses that weren't doing well for fear of slipping through the cracks entirely. From a poor rural family himself, Wallace Delois Wattles would not have escaped such fears."*

If you are reading this and are working at creating a better life for you and your family and your friends, or maybe you are just feeling down, frustrated and hopeless about your own financial situation, know this: **I get it.**

I'm not writing this as someone who is sitting pretty on a yacht in the Caribbean. I'm writing this as someone who is building every day, working to create value and products and services for the world around me, and it takes time to see any real progress or growth. I'm saying this as someone who, at the time of this writing, has a substantial amount of student loan debt that can often feel like I'll never pay it off.

However, I felt that same way about my credit card debt when I first read the book you now hold in your hands. And that credit card debt now is completely paid off.

Financial freedom starts first in your mind and with the way that you look at the world around you. This book will help with that first step.

In many ways I can say I am much "richer" now than I was before I first came across this book - from a financial standpoint and otherwise.

It isn't because there is some magical, mystical, ethereal and unknowable thing you have to figure out in order to see more "riches" come to you.

It's because the first step to really being "rich" is recognizing the wealth that is already yours and being thankful for what you do have, right where you are.

Once you start with gratitude, creativity flows naturally...and from there comes an infinite number of ideas that you can use to create wealth and a better life for you and your loved ones.

The amount of work that is required to really see lasting personal and professional change is not something that a lot of people are too keen to talk about. It forces you to come face to face with the cold, hard reality of whatever situation you may be dealing with.

You might be facing a mountain of debt or troubles - from medical bills, student loans, credit cards, child support payments, poor financial decisions from when you were younger, mortgage payments, etc.

Whatever the cause, it doesn't matter.

What you will find as you work through the material in this book and test out the concepts for yourself is that no matter what you are dealing with, **you are ultimately the one who is in control of how you respond to the situations you're facing.**

You can always learn.

You can always get better.

You can always improve.

You can always practice.

The practice is the point. **When you stop trying to "arrive" somewhere, you are immediately free to just create.**

At some point, with experience and patience, and after more practice than you can count *(because you've stopped counting)*, you will arrive at the goals you set for yourself.

If you don't set those goals first and start working towards them, they're just never going to happen. It's really that simple.

So what are you waiting for?

An invitation? Consider this one.

You have permission.

GO.

Remember:

Any new endeavor takes time and practice. Lots, and lots, and lots of practice.

Give yourself the grace to be okay with that.

Thank you for reading.

I wish you well on your creative journey.

ACTION IS THE ANTIDOTE TO DESPAIR.

- Joan Baez -

FOREWORD BY WALLACE D. WATTLES

This book is pragmatic, not philosophical. It is a practical manual, not a study of theories. It is intended for the men and women whose most pressing need is for money - for those who wish to get rich first, and philosophize afterward.

It is for those who have, so far, found neither the time, the means, nor the opportunity to go deeply into the study of metaphysics. It is for those who want results and are willing to take the conclusions of science as a basis for action, without going into all the processes by which those conclusions were reached.

It is expected that the reader will take the fundamental statements upon faith, just as you would take statements concerning a law of electrical action if they were stated by a Marconi or an Edison. It is yours to take the statements upon faith, and you will prove their truth by acting upon them without fear or hesitation.

Every man or woman who does this will certainly get rich, for the science herein applied is an exact science, and failure is impossible.

***RJR:** As with anything, it is imperative to test things out and see what works for you. Don't burn yourself out by spending a bunch of energy trying to make sure you're right all the time. A huge part of the creative process as well as the "science of getting rich," is, as I understand it, about taking your time and trying new things even if at first they may seem out of your comfort zone.*

As it pertains to taking the author's word on faith, you have to decide for yourself what works for you, what doesn't, and assessing the risks involved in doing so. I do not make so bold a claim as Wattles does as it pertains to finances, but I know for sure that much of what is in this book has helped me make a great deal of money over time. Take that for what it's worth.

For the benefit, however, of those who wish to investigate philosophical theories and so secure a logical basis for faith, I will here cite certain authorities.

The monastic theory of the universe - the theory that One is All, and that All is One; that one Substance manifests itself as the seeming many elements of the material world - is of Hindu origin, and has been gradually winning its way into the thought of the western world for two hundred years.

It is the foundation of all the Oriental philosophies, and of those of Descartes, Spinoza, Leibnitz, Schopenhauer, Hegel, and Emerson.

The reader who wants to dig into the philosophical foundations of this is advised to read Hegel and Emerson for themselves.

In writing this book I have sacrificed all other considerations to plainness and simplicity of style, so that all might understand.

The plan of action laid down herein was deduced from the conclusions of philosophy. It has been thoroughly tested, and bears the supreme test of practical experiment: it works.

If you wish to know how the conclusions were arrived at, read the writings of the authors mentioned above. If you wish to reap the fruits of their philosophies in actual practice, read this book and do exactly as it tells you to do.

- Wallace D. Wattles

RJR: *The original author of this work is very confident of his methods, as you can see. As I've mentioned and will continue to mention, it is probably best for you to try things out and see what works for you.*

No need to stress yourself out or do anything stupid.

SUCCESS USUALLY COMES TO THOSE WHO ARE TOO BUSY TO BE LOOKING FOR IT.

- Henry David Thoreau -

CHAPTER 1: THE RIGHT TO BE RICH

Whatever may be said in praise of poverty, the fact remains that it is not possible to live a really complete or successful life unless one is rich.

No person can rise to their greatest possible height in talent or soul development unless they have plenty of money; for to unfold the soul and to develop talent they must have many things to use, and they cannot have these things unless they have money to buy them with.

People develop in mind, soul, and body by making use of things, and society is so organized that humanity must have money in order to become the possessor of things. Therefore, the basis of all advancement for humanity must be the science of getting rich.

The object of all life is development. Everything that lives has an inalienable right to all the development it is capable of attaining.

Humanity's right to life means the right to have the free and unrestricted use of all the things which may be necessary to one's fullest mental, spiritual, and physical unfoldment; or, in other words, one's right to be rich.

In this book, I shall not speak of riches in a figurative way; to be really rich does not mean to be satisfied or contented with a little.

No person ought to be satisfied with a little if they are capable of using and enjoying more.

The purpose of nature is the advancement and unfoldment of life.

Every person should have all that can contribute to the power, elegance, beauty, and richness of life.

The individual who owns all they want for the living of all the life they are capable of living is rich. No one can have all that they want without plenty of money.

Life has advanced so far and become so complex that even the most ordinary man or woman requires a great amount of wealth in order to live in a manner that even approaches completeness.

Every person naturally wants to become all that they are capable of becoming — this desire to realize innate possibilities is inherent in human nature; we cannot help wanting to be all that we can be.

Success in life is becoming what you want to be. You can become what you want to be only by making use of things, and you can have the free use of things only as you become rich enough to buy them.

To understand the science of getting rich is therefore the most essential of all knowledge.

There is nothing wrong in wanting to get rich. The desire for riches is really the desire for a richer, fuller, and more abundant life - and that desire is praiseworthy.

The individual who does not desire to live more abundantly is not common. Those who do not desire to have money enough to buy all they want is out of the ordinary indeed.

There are three motives for which we live:

- We live for the body

- We live for the mind

- We live for the soul

No one of these is better or holier than the other - all of these are desirable, and no one of the three - body, mind, or soul - can live fully if either of the others is cut short of full life and expression.

It is not right or noble to live only for the soul and deny mind or body. It is wrong to live for the intellect and deny body or soul.

We are all acquainted with the loathsome consequences of living for the body and denying both mind and soul. We see that real life means the complete expression of all that someone can give forth through body, mind, and soul.

Whatever one can say, no individual can be really happy or satisfied unless their body is living fully in every function, and unless the same is true of their mind and soul.

Wherever there is unexpressed possibility or function not performed, there is unsatisfied desire.

Desire is possibility seeking expression, or function seeking performance.

You *cannot* live fully in your body without good food, comfortable clothing, warm shelter, and freedom from excessive toil. Rest and recreation are also *necessary* to your physical life.

You cannot live fully in your mind without books (and time to study them), opportunity for travel and observation, or without intellectual companionship.

To live fully in mind you must have intellectual recreations, and you must surround yourself with all the objects of art and beauty that you are capable of using and appreciating.

To live fully in soul, you must have love, and love is denied expression by poverty.

A person's highest happiness is often found in the bestowal of gifts on those they love.

Love finds its most natural and spontaneous expression in giving.

The person who has nothing to give cannot fill their place as a husband/father, wife/mother, or citizen of their community and country.

It is in the use of material things that you find full life for your body, develop your mind, and unfold your soul. It is therefore of supreme importance to you that you should be rich.

It is perfectly right that you should desire to be rich. If you are a normal man or woman you cannot help doing so. It is perfectly right that you should give your best attention to the science of getting rich, for it is the noblest and most necessary of all studies.

If you neglect this study, you are derelict in your duty to yourself, to God and humanity; for you can render to God and humanity no greater service than to make the most of yourself.

__RJR:__ Derelict can be defined here as 'in a very poor condition as a result of disuse and neglect'. Do not take this as a personal insult.

The author is merely trying to convey that it is very difficult, if not impossible, to do all of the things that you want to do if you do not have the financial means to do so.

If you just stop and think about this, you should find that it is merely a statement of fact, not a personal attack on your character or anything of that sort. We all have basic physical, mental, and emotional needs, and if any of these are withheld, there is much suffering. More often than not, the reason for those sufferings boils down to the lack of finances.

The goal is not to think that more money will make you happy, but to realize that by creating more sustainable income for yourself that you will have more freedom to do the things that make you happy.

SUCCESS CONSISTS OF GOING FROM FAILURE TO FAILURE WITH NO LOSS OF ENTHUSIASM.

- Winston Churchill -

CHAPTER 2: THERE IS A SCIENCE OF GETTING RICH

There is a science of getting rich, and it is an exact science, like algebra or arithmetic.

There are certain laws which govern the process of acquiring riches. Once these laws are learned and obeyed by any person, they will get rich with mathematical certainty.

The ownership of money and property comes as a result of doing things in a certain way. Those who do things in this certain way, whether on purpose or accidentally, get rich - while those who do not do things in this certain way, no matter how hard they work or how able they are, remain poor.

It is a natural law that like causes always produce like effects. Therefore, any man or woman who learns to do things in this certain way will infallibly get rich.

That the above statement is true is shown by the following facts:

Getting rich is not a matter of environment.

If it were, all the people in certain neighborhoods would become wealthy. The people of one city would all be rich, while those of other towns would all be poor, or the inhabitants of one state would roll in wealth, while those of an adjoining state would be in poverty.

Everywhere we see rich and poor living side by side, in the same environment, and often engaged in the same vocations. When two people are in the same locality, and in the same business, and one gets rich while the other remains poor, it shows that getting rich is not, *primarily*, a matter of environment.

Some environments may be more favorable than others, but when two people in the same business are in the same neighborhood, and one gets rich while the other fails, it indicates that getting rich is the result of doing things in a certain way.

And further, the ability to do things in this certain way is not due solely to the possession of talent, for many people who have great talent remain poor, while others who have very little talent get rich.

Studying the people who have gotten rich, we find that they are an average lot in all respects, having no greater talents and abilities than other people. It is evident that they do not get rich because they possess talents and abilities that other people don't have, but *because they happen to do things in a certain way.*

RJR: *Obviously, I am not naive to the fact that there are people who are born into extreme, abject poverty and in very dire situations that dramatically affect their financial state as well as their well-being. What I believe the author is getting at is that there are certain principles of the creative process and learning how to add value to the marketplace that will work regardless of your environment or circumstances.*

Getting rich is not the result of saving, or "thrift". Many very penurious people are poor, while free spenders often get rich.

Nor is getting rich due to doing things which others fail to do. Two people in the same business often do almost exactly the same things, and one gets rich while the other remains poor or becomes bankrupt.

From all these things, we must come to the conclusion that getting rich is the result of doing things in a certain way.

If getting rich is the result of doing things in a certain way, and if like causes always produce like effects, then any man or woman who can do things in that way can become rich, and the whole matter is brought within the domain of exact science.

The question arises here, whether this certain way may be so difficult that only a few may follow it.

This cannot be true so far as natural ability is concerned. Talented people get rich, and blockheads get rich. Intellectually brilliant people get rich, and very stupid people get rich.

Physically strong people get rich, and weak and sickly people get rich.

Some degree of ability to think and understand is, of course, essential - but as far as natural ability is concerned, any man or woman who has sense enough to read and understand these words can certainly get rich.

Also, we have seen that it is not a matter of environment. Location counts for something - one would not go to the heart of the Sahara and expect to do successful business.

Getting rich involves the art of and the necessity of dealing with humanity, and of being where there are people to deal with.

If these people are inclined to deal in the way you want to deal, so much the better. But that is about as far as environment goes.

If anybody else in your town can get rich, so can you - and if anybody else in your state can get rich, so can you.

Again, it is not a matter of choosing some particular business or profession.

People get rich in *every* business, and in every profession, while their next door neighbors in the same vocation remain in poverty.

It is true that you will do best in a business which you like.

If you have certain talents which are well developed, you will do best in a business which calls for the exercise of those talents.

Also, you will do best in a business which is suited to your environment and location. An ice-cream parlor would do better in a warm climate than in Greenland, and a salmon fishery will succeed better in the Northwest than in Florida, where there are no salmon.

Aside from these general limitations, getting rich is not dependent upon your engaging in some particular business, but upon your learning to do things in a certain way.

RJR: *If you're reading this and feeling frustrated at this point because the author keeps harping on "a certain way" and you are asking yourself, "Yeah, yeah, but what IS that certain way?" just keep reading.* ***A lot of what this boils down to is your mindset and what you do with the time and resources that you already have at your disposal.***

If, for example, you are spending inordinate amounts of time binging on Netflix/TV, mindlessly browsing the internet/social media, or engaging in other activities that will not actually lead to you producing a profit of any kind, chances are you aren't "acting in the certain way" that will lead to the kind of wealth you may want. This isn't rocket science, of course - but how are you stewarding the time, resources and skills that you have? What are you learning? What are you DOING?

If you are now in business, and anybody else in your area is getting rich in the same business, while you are not getting rich, it is because you are not doing things in the same way that the other person is doing them.

No one is prevented from getting rich by lack of capital. True, as you get capital, the increase becomes more easy and rapid, but one who has capital is already rich, and does not need to consider how to become so.

No matter how poor you may be, if you begin to do things in a certain way, you will begin to get rich and you will begin to have capital. The getting of capital is a part of the process of getting rich, and it is a part of the result which invariably follows the doing of things in the certain way.

You may be the poorest person on the continent, and be deeply in debt. You may have neither friends, influence, nor resources, but if you begin to do things in a certain way, you must infallibly begin to get rich, for like causes must produce like effects.

If you have no capital, you can get capital.

If you are in the wrong business, you can get into the right business.

If you are in the wrong location, you can go to the right location.

You can do so by beginning in your present business and in your present location to do things in the certain way which causes success.

*RJR: I would add to this section that a simple way to think about this is to **do everything you can with what you have where you are instead of focusing on the constant pursuit of more.***

An excellent book on that specific topic is "Getting Everything You Can Out of All You've Got" by Jay Abraham. You can get that here - http://amzn.to/2kYFcJV

WELL DONE IS BETTER THAN WELL SAID.

– Benjamin Franklin –

CHAPTER 3: IS OPPORTUNITY MONOPOLIZED?

No individual is kept poor because opportunity has been taken away from them or because other people have monopolized the wealth and put a fence around it.

You may be shut off from engaging in business in certain lines, or choose to not do business in certain arenas, but there are other channels open to you.

It is quite true that if you are an office worker working for a giant corporation that you have very little chance of becoming the owner of the organization in which you work; but it is also true that if you will start to act in a certain way, you can soon leave your employer and start your own business endeavors.

There is great opportunity at this time for those who will cultivate their desired skills; such people will certainly get rich. You may say that it is impossible for you to do so, but when you act upon your vision and remain consistent, you will see the success you pursue.

At different periods of human history, the tide of opportunity flows in different directions according to the needs of the whole and the particular stage of social evolution which has been reached.

Today, opportunity is open before you. It is open before the person who learns to tap into their creativity and act upon it. There is abundance of opportunity for the person who will go with the tide, instead of trying to swim against it. Employees, either as individuals or as "the working class", are not often directly deprived of opportunity. The workers are not being "kept down" by their masters; they are not being forced to stay down or remain employed by the giant corporations and business conglomerates.

As a class, they are where they are because they do not do things in a certain way. If "the working class" chose to do so, they could follow the example of many others throughout history who have built their own successful organizations through perseverance, trial and error, and cooperating with others with similar vision and values.

They could elect people of their own class to office, and pass laws favoring the development of more cooperative industries and in a few years they could take peaceable possession of the business and industrial fields.

The working class may become the master class whenever they will begin to do things in a certain way. The law of wealth is the same for them as it is for all others.

The average worker will remain exactly where they are until they begin thinking and acting differently.

The individual worker, however, is not held down by the ignorance or the mental slothfulness of his class. They can follow the tide of opportunity to riches, and this book will tell them how.

RJR: *It is definitely a bit of a mental hurdle for a lot of people to process what Wattles is saying here. It requires one to consider the fact that if they are in the employ of an organization that treats them poorly, they are, in fact, free to quit and set out on their own. He is not implying that it is an easy road - simply that no one is forced to remain in an employment situation with which they are genuinely unhappy (except in obviously extreme circumstances).*

I do not believe the author is attempting to tell you what specific type of industry you should consider going into. I believe he is suggesting that you not stress out so much in trying to build something in a heavily competitive arena and instead focus your attention more on areas of interest to you and things that would not involve unnecessary competition. Two excellent books on this topic are "Purple Cow" by Seth Godin and "Blue Ocean Strategy" by W. Chan Kim and Renée Mauborgne.

You will notice throughout this book that Wattles suggests repeatedly to stay mentally on the creative plane, not the competitive one. More on this later.

No one is kept in poverty by a shortness in the supply of riches. There is more than enough for all.

A palace as large as the capitol at Washington might be built for every family on earth from the building material in the United States alone. Under intensive cultivation, this country would produce wool, cotton, linen, and silk enough to clothe and feed each person in the world quite well.

The visible supply is practically inexhaustible, and the invisible supply really IS inexhaustible.

RJR: *Just a heads up, this is around where some folks might scoff at the concepts in this book and things may get a bit "woo-woo" for some people. I would encourage you to keep reading despite any of those frustrations, as I dealt with them myself when I first read this book. If it doesn't resonate with you, no worries. There is a lot of good content and perspectives to consider that have proved useful for me over the years.*

Thinking about this like you are simply working with your imagination has been one way to ponder these things that has been less "woo-woo" and more practical. When he speaks of "original substance" and "formless substance", if that feels too weird for you, try just replacing it with "matter", "universal energy," or something along those lines in the scientific sense.

Additionally, if you want to look at it from a spiritual standpoint, you likely can look at tapping into your creative power as a way of connecting with and honoring God as Creator.

Everything you see on earth is made from one original formless substance, out of which all things proceed.

New forms are constantly being made, and older ones are dissolving, but all are shapes made up of one thing. There is no limit to the supply of formless stuff or original substance.

The universe is made out of it, but it was not all used up in making the universe. The spaces in, through, and between the forms of the visible universe are permeated and filled with the original substance with the raw creative material of all things.

Ten thousand times more things than those that already exist might still be made, and even then we should not have exhausted the supply of universal raw material. No person, therefore, is poor because nature is poor or because there is not enough to go around.

Nature is an inexhaustible storehouse of riches. The supply will never run short. The original substance is alive with creative energy, and is constantly producing more forms. When the supply of building material is exhausted, more will be produced. When the soil is exhausted so that food stuffs and materials for clothing will no longer grow upon it, it can be renewed or more soil will be made.

__RJR:__ Do not mistake this concept as an excuse to set aside the responsibility we have a species to properly steward our natural resources on this planet. As much as it depends on us, I believe we should do so in an environmentally responsible way. I for one am all for creating sustainable, clean energy and production solutions, and doing all that we can to solve the myriad of crises that previous generations of greed and disregard for the planet have created.

When all the gold and silver has been dug from the earth, if humanity is still in such a stage of social development that we need gold and silver, more will produced from the formless. The formless stuff responds to the needs of humanity; it will not let them be without any good thing. This is true of humanity collectively. The race as a whole is always abundantly rich, and if individuals are poor, it is because they do not follow the certain way of doing things which makes the individual person rich.

RJR: *Again, if you are in a particularly bad financial situation or were born into abject poverty, do not read this as an attack on you or as disregarding how difficult your life currently is or has been. Wattles is simply saying that regardless of location or circumstance, there are certain principles that, if followed, will eventually lead one to a better quality of life.*

The formless substance is intelligent. It is substance which thinks. It is alive, and is always impelled toward more life. It is the natural and inherent impulse of life to seek to live more. It is the nature of intelligence to enlarge itself and of consciousness to seek to extend its boundaries and find fuller expression. The universe of forms has been made by a formless living substance, throwing itself into various forms in order to express itself more fully.

The universe is a great living presence, always moving inherently toward more life and fuller functioning. Nature is formed for the advancement of life. Its impelling motive is the increase of life.

For this cause, everything which can possibly minister to life is bountifully provided. There can be no lack unless God is to contradict himself and nullify his own works.

You are not kept poor by lack in the supply of riches. It is a fact which I shall demonstrate a little farther on that even the resources of the formless supply are at the command of the man or woman who will act and think in a certain way.

RJR: *Noticing the theme yet? In simple terms, making money and growing your base of wealth is all about tapping into your own inherent creative power and bringing things of value into this world that others will buy and/or pay you for.*

This is ALL work - but you're already working anyway, so why not work towards creating something of unique value that you believe in? Remember - always do what you can with what you have where you are.

NEVER MISTAKE MOTION FOR ACTION.

- ERNEST HEMINGWAY -

CHAPTER 4: THE FIRST PRINCIPLE IN THE SCIENCE OF GETTING RICH

Thought is the only power which can produce tangible riches from formless substance. The stuff from which all things are made is a substance which thinks, and imagining some type of form in this substance can lead to producing the form.

Original substance moves according to its thoughts. Every form and process and object that you see in nature is the visible expression of a thought that has been applied to some original and formless substance.

As the formless stuff thinks of a form, it takes that form. As it thinks of a motion, it makes that motion. That is the way all things were created. We live in a thought world, which is part of a thought universe.

RJR: To elaborate on this concept, especially if it feels kind of weird to think about, look at it like this: you need to first imagine/form the thought in your mind of a blue duck before you can paint a blue duck on an empty (formless) canvas (substance).

Another example: you need to first think about the shape you want to create in a piece of pottery before you can actually begin to bring form to that piece of clay. See? 'Formless substance' really can boil down to just about any kind of blank document, an empty canvas or room, a blank piece of paper, or a lump of clay. Once you apply your own imagination to work upon that 'formless substance', the creative magic starts to happen.

The thought of a moving universe extended throughout formless substance *(empty space)* and the thinking stuff moving according to that thought took the form of systems of planets and to this day maintains that form.

Thinking substance takes the form of its thought and moves according to those thoughts. Holding the idea of a circling system of suns and worlds, it takes the form of these bodies, and moves them as it thinks. Thinking of the form of a slow-growing oak tree, it moves accordingly and produces the tree, though centuries may be required to do the work.

In creating, the formless substance seems to move according to the lines of motion it has established. **The thought of an oak tree does not cause the instant formation of a full-grown tree, but it does start in motion the forces which will produce the tree along established lines of growth.**

Every thought of a form held in thinking substance causes the creation of the form, usually along the lines of growth and action already established.

If you had the thought of a particular style of house and impressed that thought upon a formless substance, it might not cause the instant formation of the house...but it would cause the turning of creative energies already working in trade and commerce into such channels, which would eventually result in the building of the house.

RJR: *Along these lines, it is impossible that Mr. Wattles would have thought about the technological advances of things like 3D printing. We truly do live in an era where if you can dream it up and design it, there is technology available that would make the creation of your ideas happen astronomically faster than in Wattles' day.*

There are already places that are 3D printing houses in a single day - (https://www.youtube.com/watch?v=wCzS2FZoB-I). The biggest encouragement I can give you is to learn as much as you can about harnessing the creative process and bringing your own ideas to life. It will serve you well in the future AND it's so much fun.

If there were no existing channels through which the creative energy could work, then the house would be formed directly from primal substance without waiting for the slow processes of the organic and inorganic world.

No thought of a form can be impressed upon original substance without causing the creation of the form.

Humanity is a thinking center and can originate thought. All the forms that humanity fashions with their hands must first exist in their minds. One cannot shape a thing until one has thought of that thing.

So far humanity has confined their efforts wholly to the work of their hands; they have applied manual labor to the world of forms, seeking to change or modify those already existing.

Many have never thought of trying to cause the creation of new forms by impressing their thoughts upon formless substances.

When you have an idea, you take material from the forms of nature and make an image of the idea (or form) which is in your mind. You have, so far, made little or no effort to cooperate with the formless intelligence; to work "with the Father".

You have not dreamed that you can "do what you see the Father doing."

***RJR:** This is a reference to a statement attributed to Jesus in John 5:19. Religious beliefs aside, it is an interesting perspective to consider. Either way, try not to get caught up in the dogma or super-spiritual sounding nature of this portion of the book and look at it like working with your imagination and the creative power we all inherently have within us.*

There are great mysteries about how we got here and spirituality that have been hotly debated for thousands of years. I am not interested in that. What I'm interested in is how we can tap into our own creativity here and now and use it to make the world a better place than we found it.

Humanity reshapes and modifies existing forms by manual labor. Few have given much attention to the question whether they may not produce things from formless substance by communicating their thoughts to it.

I propose to prove that you may do this, to prove that any man or woman may do this, and to show you how.

As our first step, we must lay down some fundamental propositions.

First, we assert that there is one original formless stuff, or substance, from which all things are made.

RJR: As mentioned earlier, if this seems weird or confusing, replace the phrase "formless stuff/substance" with "matter," "atoms," or "energy" in the scientific sense.

All the seemingly many elements are but different presentations of one element. All the many forms found in organic and inorganic nature are but different shapes, made from the same stuff.

This stuff is thinking stuff. A thought held in it produces the form of the thought.

Applying your thoughts to formless substances produces shapes.

Humanity is a thinking center, capable of original thought. If humanity can communicate their thoughts to the original thinking substance, they can cause the creation, or formation, of the things they think about.

RJR: In this sense, I would add that sitting around and just thinking about things that you want to create is not nearly as effective as thinking about the things that you want to create and actually taking practical action to make that happen. A lot of people can get tripped up on this kind of book because they perceive that those who advocate reading them are insinuating that it's just some "name it and claim it" concept or "new age thinking."

*I am of the opinion that without adding the element of **taking action** that few things actually get done in the pursuit of your goals. For example, sitting in a room at some Himalayan retreat center and thinking about writing a book is not going to magically produce the book that you want to write. You have to actually sit down and write the book!*

*It's great to first have those initial and original thoughts - however, it is what you **do** with those thoughts that will determine what happens next.*

To summarize this:

- There is a thinking stuff from which all things are made, and which, in its original state, permeates, penetrates, and fills the interspaces of the universe.

- A thought in this substance produces the thing that is imagined by the thought.

- Humanity can form things in their thoughts, and by impressing their thoughts upon formless substance can cause the things they think about to be created.

It may be asked if I can prove these statements and without going into details, I answer that I can do so, both by logic and experience.

Reasoning back from the phenomena of form and thought, I come to one original thinking substance and reasoning forward from this thinking substance, I come to humanity's power to cause the formation of the thing they think about. By experiment, I find the reasoning true, and this is my strongest proof.

If one person who reads this book gets rich by doing what it tells them to do, that is evidence in support of my claim. If every person who does what it tells them to do gets rich, that is positive proof until some one goes through the process and fails. The theory is true until the process fails, and this process will not fail, for every person who does exactly what this book tells them to do will get rich*.

RJR: **Reminder/disclaimer: I make no such claim. I **do** believe that if you take a lot of the principles in this book about the creative process and apply it to your life and your own business endeavors that it can (and often will) lead to great success. However, that is not without a large amount of work and personal and professional development. In other words, "results may vary."*

I have said that humanity gets rich by doing things in a certain way and in order to do so, humanity must learn to think in a certain way.

A person's way of doing things is the direct result of the way they think about things.

To do things in the way you want to do them, you will have to acquire the ability to think the way you want to think. This is the first step toward getting rich.

To think what you want to think is to think truth regardless of appearances.

Every person has the natural and inherent power to think what they want to think, but it requires far more effort to do so than it does to think the thoughts which are suggested by appearances. To think according to appearance is easy; to think truth regardless of appearances is laborious and often requires the expenditure of more power than any other work humanity is called upon to perform.

There is no labor from which most people shrink as they do from that of sustained and consecutive thought. It is the hardest work in the world. This is especially true when truth is contrary to appearances. Every appearance in the visible world tends to produce a corresponding form in the mind which observes it, and this can only be prevented by holding the thought of the truth.

To look upon the appearance of disease will produce the form of disease in your own mind and ultimately in your body, unless you hold the thought of the truth, which is that there is no disease - it is only an appearance, and the reality is health.

To look upon the appearances of poverty will produce corresponding forms in your own mind, unless you hold to the truth that there is no poverty, there is only abundance.

***RJR:** Here is another area that a lot of people can get tripped up - especially if all you do is look around at the state of the world today. There is plenty* of disease, poverty, lack, fear, wars, and things of that sort that would certainly seem to contradict Wattles' statements here.

Instead of getting stuck on that, try to look at it like this: we've all had those scenarios where we feel a random pain somewhere in our body and then go looking around the internet to try and figure out what it might be. We end up on a myriad of different websites and in no time we are convinced that we have stage IV cancer, diabetes, and some rare disease that we didn't even know existed until ten minutes ago, all because we spent just a short amount of time "looking upon the appearance of disease".

The statistical odds of **actually** having those diseases is - at least in most cases - very, very small - but the likelihood of instilling vast amounts of fear in our minds after looking at all of that stuff is very, very high. Fear and stress can lead to all kinds of diseases, which is why it's not advisable to waste your time or mental energy looking at those kinds of things and worrying about it.

If you are genuinely concerned about your health, go and see a licensed and trusted medical doctor. Don't go browsing around the internet looking for self-diagnoses. Rarely does that go well for anyone.

I would say the same about financial struggles and poverty. If you are in a dire financial situation, spending all your time and energy fretting about it does you no good. Instead, **choose** - (yes, it's a choice) - to read and learn all you can on how to better manage your finances.

Learn from those who have attained the kind of financial success that you seek. Use your creative energies to invest in your potential and learn everything you can about how to better tap into the vast sources of abundance that this world has to offer.

You can **choose** to do this instead of stressing yourself out about your current financial state or the financial state of others on the other side of the world. It takes practice - a lot of it - but the pay off is worth it.

The best thing you can do for others in a state of poverty is to teach them how to get out of it. If you are in poverty yourself, the best thing you can *do is to learn how to get out of it...not to sit and lament over how broke you are. It **will** take time and dedicated effort - often more time than any of us would like - but there are countless mentors, stories, biographies, and videos that you can learn from on how to get out of bad financial situations. There are also often community resources that may be of help to you. Ask around and use the internet to find the assistance you need.*

Know this: *I deeply understand how it feels to not know where your next rent check is coming from or how you're going to keep food on the table. I know what it's like to have to depend on gifts and handouts from others when money is tight. It is not fun, but it is also not permanent...not if you choose to devote yourself to getting out of it and put in the work required to do so. You've got this. Keep going.*

It takes power and diligence to think and meditate about health when surrounded by the appearances of disease or to think and meditate about riches when in the midst of appearances of poverty. However, those who acquire and cultivate this power become MASTER MINDS. They can conquer fate and have what they want.

This power can only be acquired by getting hold of the basic fact which is behind all appearances: that fact is that there is one thinking substance from which and by which all things are made.

We must grasp the truth that every thought or idea held in this substance can become a form. Humanity can impress their thoughts upon formless substances, bring form to them, and turn what once was formless into visible things.

When we realize this, we lose all doubt and fear, for **we know that we can create what we want to create, that we can get what we want to have, and that we can become what we want to be.**

As a first step toward getting rich, you must believe the three fundamental statements given previously in this chapter, and in order to emphasize them, I repeat them here:

- There is a thinking stuff from which all things are made, and which, in its original state, permeates, penetrates, and fills the interspaces of the universe.

- A thought in this substance produces the thing that is imagined by the thought.

- Humanity can form things in their thoughts, and by impressing their thoughts upon formless substance can cause the things they think about to be created.

You must lay aside all other concepts of the universe than this one. You must dwell upon this until it is fixed in your mind and has become your habitual, subconscious thought.

Read these creed statements over and over again. Fix every word upon your memory and meditate upon them until you firmly believe what they say.

If a doubt comes to you, cast it aside. Do not listen to arguments against this idea. Do not go to churches or lectures where a contrary concept of things is taught or preached. Do not read magazines, newspapers or books which teach a different idea. If you get mixed up in your faith, all your efforts will be in vain.

Do not ask why these things are true, nor speculate as to how they can be true, simply take them on trust. The science of getting rich begins with the absolute acceptance of this faith.

RJR: *As I've said elsewhere, I would not advise blind allegiance to any creed or concept as Wattles suggests above. Test everything out for yourself as a scientist would. I have found that a lot of the concepts in this book have been helpful in my journey, but I would not turn it into a religion/ dogma and insist that people just fall in line and believe me. Try and see what works, and then keep doing what works for you.*

ACTION WILL REMOVE THE DOUBTS THAT THEORY CANNOT SOLVE.

- Tehyi Hsieh -

CHAPTER 5: INCREASING LIFE

You must get rid of the last vestige of the old idea that there is a deity whose will it is that you should be poor or whose purposes may be served by keeping you in poverty.

The intelligent substance which is in all things and lives in everything also lives in you. It is a consciously living substance. Being a consciously living substance, it must have the nature and inherent desire of every living intelligence for the increase of life.

Every living thing must continually seek for the enlargement of its life because life - in the mere act of living - must increase itself.

When a seed is dropped into the ground, it springs into activity. In the act of living, it produces hundreds or thousands more seeds. Life, by living and by definition, multiplies itself.

It is forever becoming more; it must do so, if it continues to be at all.

Intelligence is under this same necessity for continuous increase. Every thought we think makes it necessary for us to think another thought. Our consciousness is continually expanding.

Every fact we learn leads us to the learning of another fact. Knowledge is continually increasing.

Every talent that we cultivate brings to the mind the desire to cultivate another talent. We are subject to the urge of life. While seeking the expression of that urge, we are driven to know more, to do more, and to be more.

In order to know more, do more, and be more we must have more. We must have things to use. Why? Because we learn, and do, and become, only by using things. Therefore, we must get rich so that we can live more.

The desire for riches is simply the capacity for larger life seeking fulfillment. Every desire is the effort of an unexpressed possibility to come into action.

It is power seeking to manifest which causes desire. That which makes you want more money is the same as that which makes the plant grow. It is life, and it is seeking fuller expression.

The one living substance must be subject to this inherent law of all life. It is permeated with the desire to live more and that is why it is under the necessity of creating things.

Since this desire to live and express more is also within you, it wants you to have all the things you can use.

RJR: *The fact that you are even reading this book is proof of this concept. You would not be reading a book called 'The Science of Getting Rich' if you did not have some inherent desire for more wealth, more freedom to express yourself, and more freedom to do the things that wealth provides. However, do not mistakenly think that simply having more money will make you happier.*

While making sure that your basic needs are met is oftentimes a source of great unrest and it is a huge relief when those financial problems are no more, lasting happiness is not something that occurs just because you have more money in the bank.

Happiness is an internal state and most times is the result of choices that we make, perspectives we adopt about our circumstances, the actions we take, and the kinds of people we surround ourselves with. There are plenty of stories of very exceedingly wealthy people who are miserable, depressed, and many who end up alone and with broken families because of their own issues with greed, deception, and things of that sort. To explore this concept further, another excellent book to pick up is 'The Soul of Money' by Lynn Twist.

It is the desire of God that you should get rich. God wants you to get rich because he can express himself better through you if you have plenty of things to use in giving him expression. He can live more in you if you have unlimited command of the means of life.

The universe desires you to have everything you want to have.

Nature is friendly to your plans. Everything is naturally for you. Make up your mind that this is true.

It is essential, however that your purpose should harmonize with the purpose that is in all things.

You must want real life, not mere pleasure or sensual gratification. Life is the performance of function, and the individual really lives only when they perform every function (physical, mental, and spiritual) of which they are capable, without excess in any.

You do not want to get rich in order to live swinishly for the gratification of animal desires. That is not life. However, the performance of every physical function is a part of life, and no one lives completely who denies the impulses of the body a normal and healthy expression.

You do not want to get rich solely to enjoy mental pleasures, to get knowledge, to gratify ambition, to outshine others, or to be famous. All of these are a legitimate part of life, but the person who lives for the pleasures of the intellect alone will only have a partial life, and they will never be satisfied with their lot.

You do not want to get rich solely for the good of others, to lose yourself for the salvation of mankind, to experience the joys of philanthropy and sacrifice. The joys of the soul are only a part of life, and they are no better or nobler than any other part.

You want to get rich in order that you may eat, drink, and be merry when it is time to do these things. You want to get rich in order that you may surround yourself with beautiful things, see distant lands, feed your mind, and develop your intellect.

You want to be rich so that you may love those around you and those you care about, do kind things, and be able to play a good part in helping the world to find truth.

Just remember that extreme altruism is no better and no nobler than extreme selfishness - both are mistakes.

Get rid of the idea that God wants you to sacrifice yourself for others, and that you can secure his favor by doing so. God requires nothing of the kind.

What God wants is that you should make the most of yourself, for yourself, and for others. You can help others by making the most of yourself more than in any other way.

You can make the most of yourself only by getting rich, so it is right and praiseworthy that you should give your first and best thought to the work of acquiring wealth.

***RJR:** Keep in mind here that the author is not suggesting that the end-all, be-all is financial gain. That is not the point. The point is that without having our basic financial needs met and having enough material wealth in order to do the things that we have in our hearts to do, we end up striving and struggling in our creative pursuits. When that is the case, often people end up getting stuck in the competitive, not the creative mind.*

It is only once we overcome our fear of not having enough or being enough that we truly are able to lean into our creative power and operate from that place.

Remember, however, that the desire of the universe is for all, and its movements must be for more life to all. It cannot be made to work for less life to any, because it is equally in all, seeking riches and life.

The intelligent substance will make things for you, but it will not take things away from someone else and give them to you.

You must get rid of the thought of competition. You are to create, not to compete for what is already created. You do not have to take anything away from any one. You do not have to drive sharp bargains.

You do not have to cheat, or to take advantage. You do not need to let anyone work for you for less than they earn.

You do not have to covet the property of others, or to look at it with wishful eyes. No one has anything of which you cannot have the like, and you can do so without taking what they have away from them.

You are to become a creator, not a competitor.

No other creature on earth has been granted the creative abilities that you have, and when you learn to harness that creative power, you tap into something beyond yourself.

You are going to get what you want, but you will get it in such a way that when you get it, every other person will have more than they have now. I am aware that there are those who get a vast amount of money by proceeding in direct opposition to the statements in the paragraph above, and want to add a word of explanation here.

There are those of the plutocratic and competitive type who become very rich sometimes purely by their extraordinary ability on the plane of competition. Sometimes they unconsciously align themselves with the infinite substance in its great purposes and movements through their contributions to the evolution of various industries.

Rockefeller, Andrew Carnegie, JP Morgan, and those of their type have been the unconscious agents of the Supreme Powers that be in the necessary work of systematizing and organizing productive industry. In the end, their work will contribute immensely toward increased life for all.

Their day is nearly over. They have organized production, and will soon be succeeded by the agents of the multitude, who will organize the machinery of distribution.

The multi-millionaires are like the monster reptiles of the prehistoric eras. They play a necessary part in the evolutionary process, but the same power which produced them will eventually be rid of them.

It is well to bear in mind that they have never been really rich - a record of the private lives of most of this class will show that they have really been the most abject and wretched of the poor.

Riches secured on the competitive plane are never satisfactory and permanent. They are yours today and another's tomorrow. Remember: if you are to become rich in a scientific and certain way, you must rise entirely out of the competitive mindset and focus on the creative one.

You must never think for a moment that the supply is limited.

RJR: *Even in Wattles' day, there were those that today we would call "the 1%" who seemed to have an almost unbelievable amount of material wealth, control, and power. Rockefeller, Carnegie, JP Morgan, and others wielded immense influence over the way things developed in the United States especially, and undoubtedly there was a lot of not-so-nice things that they did to maintain that power.*

What Wattles is saying here is sound advice: essentially, don't stress yourself out so much about those who seem to have limitless supplies of financial wealth and power. Focus on what you can do to bring value into the world. Focus on what you can create and building your own creative endeavors. You do not need to compete in order to do this.

Just as soon as you begin to think that all the money is being "cornered" and controlled by bankers and others and that you must exert yourself to get laws passed to stop this process and so on - it is in that moment that you drop into the competitive mind.

This is where your power to cause creation is gone for the time being, and what is worse, you will probably slow down or stop the creative movements you have already begun.

RJR: *I am the first to admit that if I spend even a few minutes looking at "the news" or mindlessly browsing social media and the limitless number of articles or videos that are published every day, I can burn out and get overwhelmed very quickly. They spend so much time, energy, and money heralding all of the various types of corruption, power-grabs, and politicking that goes on in the competitive financial and political arenas.*

It often leaves me (and most people I know) feeling helpless, afraid, and powerless to do anything positive in this world because, well hey - look at how terrible things can be! There is so much fear, uncertainty and finger-pointing that it renders the creative spark almost completely useless - at least until I'm able to snap out of it and get back to building what I'm working on.

This is what I believe Wattles is addressing here. It's not that you shouldn't care about the goings-on in your community or stick your head in the sand. It is that your energy and focus is best spent CREATING, not consuming all of the drama and noise of the world around you.

KNOW that there are countless millions of dollars' worth of gold in the mountains of the earth, not yet brought to light. Know that if there were not, more would be created from the thinking substance to supply your needs.

KNOW that the money you need will come, even if it is necessary for a thousand people to be led to the discovery of new gold mines tomorrow.

Never look at the visible supply - look always at the limitless riches in the formless substance, and KNOW that they are coming to you as fast as you can receive and use them. Nobody, by cornering the visible supply, can prevent you from getting what is yours.

Never allow yourself to think for an instant that all the best building spots will be taken before you get ready to build your house unless you hurry.

Never worry about the trusts and giant corporations and get anxious and fear that they will soon come to own the whole earth. Never be afraid that you will lose what you want because some other person "beats you to it."

That cannot possibly happen, for you are not seeking anything that is possessed by anybody else. You are causing what you want to be created from the formless substance, and the supply is without limits.

Stick to the basics:

- There is a thinking stuff from which all things are made, and which, in its original state, permeates, penetrates, and fills the interspaces of the universe.

- A thought in this substance produces the thing that is imagined by the thought.

- Humanity can form things in their thoughts, and by impressing their thoughts upon formless substance can cause the things they think about to be created.

RJR: Again, just a reminder here if this feels too "woo-woo" or overtly spiritual - when thinking of "formless substance", remind yourself that everything around you that you can see was first without form.

Every object that is around you right at this very moment at one time only existed in someone else's mind.

You too can harness that creative power and generate wealth for yourself.

WE ARE WHAT WE REPEATEDLY DO. EXCELLENCE, THEN, IS NOT AN ACT, BUT A HABIT.

- Aristotle -

CHAPTER 6: HOW RICHES COME TO YOU

When I say that you do not have to drive sharp bargains, I do not mean that you do not have to drive any bargains at all, or that you are above the necessity for having any dealings with your fellow person. I mean that you will not need to deal with them unfairly.

You do not have to get something for nothing, but you can give to every person more than you take from them.

You cannot give every person more in cash market value than you take from them, but you can give them more in use value than the cash value of the thing you take from them. The paper, ink, and other material in this book may not be worth the money you pay for it, but if the ideas suggested by it bring you thousands of dollars, you have not been wronged by those who sold it to you - **they have given you a great use value for a small cash value.**

Let us suppose that I own a picture by one of the great artists, which, in any civilized community, is worth thousands of dollars. I take it to Baffin Bay, and by "salesmanship" induce an Eskimo to give a bundle of furs worth $500 for it. I have really wronged him, for he has no use for the picture. **It has no use value to him and thus it will not add to his quality of life.**

But suppose I give him a gun worth $50 for his furs. In this way, he has made a good bargain. He has use for the gun - it will get him many more furs and much food, it will add to his life in every way. It will make him rich.

When you rise from the competitive to the creative plane, you can scan your business transactions very strictly, and if you are selling any person anything which does not add more to their life than the thing they give you in exchange, you can afford to stop it.

You do not have to compete or work to beat anybody in business. If you are in a business which does make you compete with people, get out of it at once.

Give everyone more in use value than you take from them in cash value. It is then that you are adding to the life of the world by every business transaction.

If you have people working for you, you must take from them more in cash value than you pay them in wages...but you can so organize your business that it will be filled with the principle of advancement. In this way, each employee who wishes to do so may advance a little every day.

You can make your business do for your employees what this book is doing for you. You can conduct your business in a way that it will be a sort of ladder by which every employee who will work towards it may climb to riches themselves. If they are given the opportunity but do not do so, it is not your fault.

Keep in mind that just because you are to cause the creation of your riches from the formless substance which permeates all of your environment, it does not mean that they will immediately take shape from the atmosphere and come into being right before your eyes.

If you want a sewing machine, for instance, I do not mean to tell you that you are to impress the thought of a sewing machine on the thinking substance until the machine is formed out of thin air in the room where you currently are. But if you want a sewing machine, hold the mental image of it with the most positive certainty that it is being made or is on its way to you.

After once forming the thought, have the most absolute and unquestioning faith that the sewing machine is coming. Never think or speak of it in any other way than being en route to you. Claim it as already yours.

It will be brought to you by the power of the supreme intelligence, acting upon the minds of humanity. If you live in Maine, it may be that someone will be brought from Texas or Japan to engage in some transaction which will result in your getting what you want.

If so, the whole matter will be as much to that person's advantage as it is to yours.

RJR: *As mentioned elsewhere, this is one of those areas of the book where people might get caught up in the whole "name it-claim it" thing. At least for me, I have tried to not get stuck on this stuff as much as just looking at it like learning how to form clear, focused goals.*

When you are setting definite goals for yourself, you obviously have to form a clear mental picture of those goals and keep believing that it is possible to achieve them in order for you to see them come to fruition. At least in my own experience, I have found that rarely do things come to me in the time frame that I would like them to (patience is not one of my favorite things) - but if I consistently pursue the goals I set for myself, eventually I do see them achieved.

This is not rocket science, of course - but I believe what Wattles is getting at is reminding you, dear reader, to not lose hope and to not give up or abandon your thoughts over to doubts and fear when in the pursuit of your goals. ***It is simply not useful.***

Do not forget for a moment that the thinking substance is in all things, communicating with everyone, and can influence everything. The desire of the thinking substance for fuller life and better living has caused the creation of all the sewing machines that have already been made and it can cause the creation of millions more. It will do this whenever people set these things in motion by desire, faith and by acting in a certain way.

You can certainly have a sewing machine in your house and it is just as certain that you can have any other things which you want which you will use for the advancement of your own life and the lives of others.

You need not hesitate about asking largely; "it is your Father's pleasure to give you the kingdom," said Jesus.

The original substance wants to live fully expressed in you and wants you to have all that you can or will use for the living of the most abundant life.

If you fix upon your consciousness the fact that the desire you feel for the possession of riches is one with the desire of God for more complete expression, your faith becomes invincible.

Once I saw a little boy sitting at a piano, and vainly trying to bring harmony out of the keys. I saw that he was grieved and provoked by his inability to play real music. I asked him the cause of his frustration, and he answered, "I can feel the music in me, but I can't make my hands go right."

The music in him was the urge of the original substance, containing all the possibilities of all life. All that there is of music was seeking expression through the child.

God, the One Substance, is trying to live and do and enjoy things through humanity. He is saying, "I want hands to build wonderful structures, to play divine harmonies, to paint glorious pictures. I want feet to run my errands, eyes to see my beauties, tongues to tell mighty truths and to sing marvelous songs," and so on.

Every possibility is seeking expression through humankind. God wants those who can play music to have pianos and every other instrument and to have the means to cultivate their talents to the fullest extent. He wants those who can appreciate beauty to be able to surround themselves with beautiful things.

He wants those who can discern truth to have every opportunity to travel and observe. He wants those who can appreciate fashion to be beautifully clothed, and those who can appreciate good food to be luxuriously fed.

He wants all these things because he enjoys and appreciates them. It is God who wants to play, sing, enjoy beauty, proclaim truth and wear fine clothes, and eat good foods. "It is God that works in you to will and to do," said Paul.

The desire you feel for riches is the infinite seeking to express itself in you as it sought to find expression in the little boy at the piano, so you need not hesitate to ask largely.

Your part is to focus and express the desire to God.

This is a difficult point with most people. They retain something of the old idea that poverty and self-sacrifice are pleasing to God. They look upon poverty as a part of the plan, a necessity of nature. They have the idea that God has finished his work and made all that he can make, and that the majority of humanity must stay poor because there is not enough to go around.

They hold to so much of this erroneous thought that they feel ashamed to ask for wealth. They try not to want more than a very modest competence... just enough to make them fairly comfortable.

RJR: *Whatever you believe regarding your faith or your religion (or lack thereof), just consider for a moment how so many of us were brought up. I have been hard pressed to find a single person who has not grown up in some kind of religious environment where the doctrine is taught very aggressively that poverty is somehow something that reflects a 'holy' or upright lifestyle.*

Anyone who has struggled with financial difficulties can tell you that it is not something that often leads to having a positive worldview or treating people well. If you are struggling with poverty, you also most likely struggle in the areas of health - physically, mentally, and emotionally. Most people often will find it difficult to appreciate much of anything if their most basic of needs are not met.

Throughout human history, religious dogma and politicking has been used to control the masses and take advantage of the poor by appealing to them to donate the little that they have to their organizations (who oftentimes are run by leaders that live very lavish lifestyles). While I certainly do not advocate living in excess and giving in to greed, I also do not adhere to the world view that any higher power would want us as a species to remain in poverty. It is not healthy and not useful to do so.

I recall now the case of one student who was told that he must get in mind a clear picture of the things he desired so that the creative thought of them might be impressed on the formless substance. He was a very poor man, living in a rented house, and having only what he earned from day to day. He could not grasp the fact that all wealth was his.

After thinking the matter over, he decided that he might reasonably ask for a new rug for the floor of his best room and a stove to heat the house during the cold weather.

Following the instructions given in this book, he obtained these things in a few months and then it dawned upon him that he had not asked enough. He went through the house in which he lived, and planned all the improvements he would like to make in it. He mentally added a bay window here and a room there until it was so complete in his mind as his ideal home that he even envisioned and planned the furnishings.

Holding the whole picture in his mind, he began living in the certain way and moving toward what he wanted. He owns the house now, and is rebuilding it after the form of his mental image. And now, with still larger faith, he is going on to get greater things.

It has been unto him according to his faith, and it is so with you and with all of us.

RJR: *Notice how in the story above that the author points out that first the man formed a clear picture of what he was wanting in his mind. So few of us even allow ourselves the luxury of imagining what our lives could be like if we were not struggling with this problem or that problem.*

By exercising the power of your imagination and allowing yourself permission to dream big, you can get a clear image of what you're wanting your life to look like. Write these things down. Keep them somewhere that you can see them like a journal or a whiteboard in your room or office.

At least for me, so much of this is about reminding myself where I want to be heading and forming clear pictures of the life I want to build. Exercising your imagination in this method is the only way I know how to do it.

SUCCESS SEEMS TO BE LARGELY A MATTER OF HANGING ON AFTER OTHERS HAVE LET GO.

- William Feather -

CHAPTER 7: GRATITUDE

The illustrations given in the last chapter will have conveyed to the reader the fact that the first step toward getting rich is to convey the idea of your wants to the formless substance.

This is true, and you will see that in order to do so it becomes necessary to relate yourself to the formless intelligence in a harmonious way.

To secure this harmonious relationship is a matter of such primary and vital importance that I shall give some space to its discussion here and give you instructions which, if you will follow them, will be certain to bring you into perfect unity of mind with God.

The whole process of mental adjustment and atonement can be summed up in one word: gratitude.

First, you believe that there is one intelligent substance, from which all things proceed. Second, you believe that this substance gives you everything you desire, and third, you relate yourself to it by a feeling of deep and profound gratitude.

Many people who order their lives rightly in all other ways are kept in poverty by their lack of gratitude. Having received one gift from God, they cut the wires which connect them with him by failing to make acknowledgments of thanksgiving.

It is easy to understand that the nearer we live to the source of wealth, the more wealth we shall receive, and it is easy also to understand that the soul that is always grateful lives in closer touch with God than the one which never looks to him in thankful acknowledgment.

The more gratefully we fix our minds on the source of everything when good things come to us, the more good things we will receive, and the more rapidly they will come.

The reason simply is that the mental attitude of gratitude draws the mind into closer touch with the source from which the blessings come. If it is a new thought to you that gratitude brings your whole mind into closer harmony with the creative energies of the universe, consider it well, and you will see that it is true.

The good things you already own have come to you along the line of obedience to certain laws of the universe.

Gratitude will lead your mind out along the ways by which things come. It will keep you in close harmony with creative thought and prevent you from falling into competitive thought.

Gratitude alone can keep you looking toward that which is infinite and prevent you from falling into the error of thinking of the supply as limited. To do that would be fatal to your hopes.

There is a law of gratitude and it is absolutely necessary that you should observe the law if you are to get the results you seek. The law of gratitude is the natural principle that action and reaction are always equal and in opposite directions.

The grateful outreaching of your mind in thankful praise to God is a liberation or expenditure of force; it cannot fail to reach that to which it is addressed, and the reaction is an instantaneous movement towards you.

"Draw near to God, and he will draw near to you."

If your gratitude is strong and constant, the reaction in the formless substance will be strong and continuous. The movement of the things you want will be always toward you. Notice the grateful attitude that Jesus took; how he always seems to be saying, "I thank you, Father, that you hear me." You cannot exercise much creative power without gratitude, for it is gratitude that keeps you connected with that creative power.

The value of gratitude does not consist solely in getting you more blessings in the future. Without gratitude, you cannot long keep from being dissatisfied regarding things as they are.

The moment you permit your mind to dwell with dissatisfaction upon things as they are, you begin to lose ground.

When you fix your attention upon the common, the ordinary, the poor, the squalid and the mean, your mind takes upon itself the form of these things. Then you will transmit these forms or mental images to the formless substance, and the common, the poor, the squalid, and mean will come to you.

To permit your mind to dwell upon the inferior is to become inferior and to surround yourself with inferior things. On the other hand, to fix your attention on the best is to surround yourself with the best, and to become the best. The creative power within us makes us into the image of that which we give our attention to. We are thinking substance, and thinking substance always takes the form of that which it thinks about.

The grateful mind is constantly fixed upon the best, therefore it tends to become the best. It takes the form or character of the best and will receive the best.

Also, faith is born of gratitude. The grateful mind continually expects good things, and that expectation becomes faith. The reaction of gratitude upon one's own mind produces faith and every outgoing wave of grateful thanksgiving increases faith.

Those who have no feeling of gratitude cannot long retain a living faith, and without a living faith you cannot get rich by the creative method, as we shall see in the following chapters.

It is necessary, then, to cultivate the habit of being grateful for every good thing that comes to you and to give thanks continuously. Because all things have contributed to your advancement, you should include all things in your gratitude. Do not waste time thinking or talking about the shortcomings or wrong actions of plutocrats or trust magnates. Their organization of the world has made your opportunity. All you get really comes to you because of them.

Do not throw yourself into a rage against corrupt politicians - if it were not for politicians we should fall into anarchy, and your opportunity would be greatly lessened. God has worked a long time and very patiently to bring us up to where we are in industry and government, and he is going right on with his work. There is not the least doubt that he will do away with plutocrats, trust magnates, captains of industry, and politicians as soon as they can be spared...but in the meantime, behold they are all needed. Remember that they are all helping to arrange the lines of transmission along which your riches will come to you, and be grateful to them all.

This will bring you into harmonious relations with the good in everything, and the good in everything will move toward you.

RJR: *Do not misinterpret the above passages to mean that you should not stand up for what you believe in or that you have to tolerate things that are done by those in authority positions that are harmful to you or others.*

It is my belief that what Wattles is saying here is to not allow it to consume so much of your mental thought and energy that you get fearful and distracted from pursuing your goals and creating the life of your dreams.

Especially in today's age of hyper-sensationalized news on every device, newspaper, screen and all over social media, it has never been more important to learn how to disconnect from the drama of the outside world and focus on what is right in front of you. Connect more with the people and things most important to you and do what you can.

Maintaining an attitude of "doing to others what you would have them do to you" is my biggest suggestion to anyone as a way to figure out how to conduct themselves and how to speak to others.

FALL SEVEN TIMES, STAND UP EIGHT.

- Japanese Proverb -

CHAPTER 8: THINKING IN THE CERTAIN WAY

Turn back to chapter 6 and read again the story of the man who formed a mental image of his house, and you will get a fair idea of the initial step toward getting rich.

You must form a clear and definite mental picture of what you want.

You cannot transmit an idea unless you have it yourself.

You must have it before you can give it, and many people fail to impress the thinking substance because they have themselves only a vague and misty concept of the things they want to do, to have, or to become.

***RJR:** Stop and think about this for a moment. Have you ever **actually** asked yourself what you really want in this life?*

*So often we get caught up in what we think we need or what our parents or spouses or loved ones or friends or family members or teachers or pastors or other authority figures want us to do for **them** that we don't think about what we actually want for **ourselves**.*

You cannot "love others as you love yourself" until you first learn to love yourself. This is not a selfish act - it is necessary in order to really achieve lasting happiness and the goals that you have. First and foremost, you must figure out what it is that you actually want. Try it and see what happens. Write "What do I really want?" on a piece of paper and jot down the answers that come to mind. You might be surprised.

It is not enough that you should have a general desire for wealth "to do good with" - everybody has that desire.

It is not enough that you should have a wish to travel, see things, live more, etc. Everybody has those desires also.

If you were going to send a message to a friend, you would not send the letters of the alphabet in their order and let him construct the message for himself, nor would you list words at random from the dictionary.

You would send a coherent sentence - one which meant something.

When you try to impress your wants upon the formless substance, remember that it must be done by a coherent statement. You must know what you want, and be definite.

You can never get rich or start the creative power into action by sending out unformed longings and vague desires.

Go over your desires just as the man I described earlier went over his house in his imagination.

Imagine just what you want and get a clear mental picture of it as you wish it to look when you get it.

That clear mental picture you must have continually in mind, as the sailor has in mind the port toward which he is sailing the ship. You must keep your face toward it all the time. You must no more lose sight of it than the captain of a ship loses sight of the compass.

RJR: One of the things that I have found to be extremely effective is creating a 'vision board'. You can do a simple web search for 'vision board' and see all kinds of examples.

It's fun and easy: get a piece of posterboard from a local department or craft store, some magazines, scissors and a glue stick - and go through the magazines cutting out images and phrases that stand out to you.

It could be simple things like encouraging words and phrases or physical items like houses, locations, and objects. I also add to my vision board things that remind me of past successes that I have had: pay stubs from large client gigs that we have landed, receipts for debts that I have paid off, etc.

The point of this exercise, though it might feel or sound silly and childish if you have never done it, is to have in your home or office a constant reminder of what you are aiming at as well as reminders of the successes you have already attained.

When things get tough (and they inevitably will at some point), that vision board is something to go back to and remind yourself what you're wanting to do, how you want your life to look, and the struggles you have already overcome. When you know WHY you are doing something, it makes it much easier to handle the HOW.

Try it - you won't regret it.

It is not necessary to take exercises in concentration, nor to set apart special times for prayer and affirmation, nor to "go into the silence," nor to do occult stunts of any kind. **All you need is to know what you want and to want it badly enough so that it will stay in your thoughts.**

Spend as much of your leisure time as you can in contemplating your mental image. No one needs to take exercises to concentrate their mind on something which they really want. It is the things you do not really care about which require effort to fix your attention upon them.

It will hardly be worthwhile for you to try to carry out the instructions given in this book unless you really want to get rich. The desire to do so must be strong enough to hold your thoughts directed to that purpose - much like the magnetic pole holds the needle of the compass.

The methods I offer here are for people whose desire for riches is strong enough to overcome mental laziness and the love of ease, and are ready to put in the work required to achieve those goals.

The more clear and definite you make your mental picture then, and the more you dwell upon it, bringing out all its delightful details, the stronger your desire will be. The stronger your desire, the easier it will be to hold your mind fixed upon the picture of what you want.

Something more is necessary, however, than merely to see the picture clearly. If that is all you do, you are only a dreamer, and will have little or no power for accomplishment.

Behind your clear vision must be the purpose to realize it and to bring it out in tangible expression. And behind this purpose must be an invincible and unwavering faith that the thing is already yours.

You must believe that it is "at hand" and you have only to take possession of it.

RJR: As I've said before - do not think Wattles is suggesting that you just sit in a room and imagine what you want all day long. Getting a clear vision of the life you want is of utmost importance - but vision without taking consistent action in the direction of those goals is simply fantasy.

Live in the new house mentally, until it takes form around you physically. In the mental realm, enter at once into full enjoyment of the things you want.

"Whatsoever things you ask for when you pray, believe that you have received them, and you shall have them," said Jesus. See the things you want as if they were actually around you all the time.

See yourself as owning and using them. Make use of them in your imagination just as you will use them when they are your tangible possessions.

Dwell upon your mental picture until it is clear and distinct, and then take the mental attitude of ownership toward everything in that picture.

Take possession of it in your mind, in the full faith that it is actually yours. Hold to this mental ownership. Do not waver for an instant in the faith that it is real.

And remember what was said in a proceeding chapter about gratitude - be as thankful for it all the time as you expect to be when it has taken form.

The person who can sincerely be thankful for the things which are currently only in their imagination has real faith. That person will get rich and can cause the creation of whatsoever they want.

You do not need to pray repeatedly for things that you want. It is not necessary to tell God about it every day.

"Do not use vain repetitions as the heathen do," said Jesus said to his pupils, "for your Father knows that you have need of these things before you ask Him."

Your part is to intelligently formulate your desire for the things which make for a larger life, and to get these desires arranged into a coherent whole. Then impress this whole desire upon the formless substance which has the power and the will to bring you what you want.

You do not make this impression by repeating strings of words. You make it by holding the vision with unshakable **purpose** to attain it, and with steadfast faith that you will attain it.

The answer to prayer is not according to your faith while you are talking, but according to your faith while you are working.

You cannot impress the mind of God by having a special sabbath day set apart to tell him what you want and then forgetting him during the rest of the week.

You cannot impress him by having special hours to go into your "prayer closet" and pray if you then dismiss the matter from your mind until the hour of prayer comes again.

Oral prayer is well enough, and has its effect - especially upon yourself in clarifying your vision and strengthening your faith - but it is not your oral petitions which get you what you want. In order to get rich you do not need a "sweet hour of prayer", you need to "pray without ceasing."

And by prayer, I mean holding steadily to your vision with the purpose to cause its creation into solid form and the faith that you are doing so.

"Believe that you have received them."

The whole matter turns on receiving, once you have clearly formed your vision. At this point, it is fine to make an oral statement, addressing God in reverent prayer. From that moment forward, you must envision in your mind what you want and believe that you will receive what you ask for.

Live in the new house. Wear the fine clothes. Ride in the automobile. Go on the journey, and confidently plan for greater journeys.

Think and speak of all the things you have asked for in terms of actual present ownership.

Imagine an environment and a financial condition exactly as you want them and live as much as you can in that imaginary environment and financial condition.

Mind, however, that you do not do this as a mere dreamer and mental castle builder: hold to the faith that the imaginary is being realized, and focus on the purpose for its realization.

Remember that it is faith and purpose in the use of the imagination which make the difference between the scientist and the dreamer.

And having learned this fact, it is here that you must learn the proper use of the will.

RJR: *I will keep reminding you throughout this book that simply envisioning what you want is not enough.*

It is a vital first step - one that many resist doing because they feel it is foolish or childish. But it is not the only step - **you must take action in the direction of your dreams***...even if that means learning how to position yourself in a way to receive them as they come.*

NOTHING DIMINISHES ANXIETY FASTER THAN ACTION.

- Walter Anderson -

CHAPTER 9: HOW TO USE THE WILL

To set about getting rich in a scientific way, do not try to apply your will power to anything outside of yourself. You have no right to do so anyway.

It is wrong to apply your will to other men and women in order to get them to do what you wish done.

It is as flagrantly wrong to coerce people by mental power as it is to coerce them by physical power.

If compelling people by physical force to do things for you reduces them to slavery, compelling them by mental means accomplishes exactly the same thing; the only difference is in methods.

RJR: There is a big difference between doing sales and marketing in a way that informs and entertains your audience about a valuable product or service that you are offering and blatant, intentional and Machiavellian manipulation.

I strongly advise against the latter. It will not make you happy in the long run, and when people realize you've been manipulating them, they will no longer trust you or purchase your products or services. You don't like it when it happens to you - so kindly reconsider when thinking about doing so to others.

If taking things from people by physical force is robbery, then taking things by mental force is robbery also. There is no difference in principle.

You have no right to use your will power upon another person, even if you believe it is "for their own good", for you do not know what would be good for them. The science of getting rich does not require you to apply power or force to any other person in any way whatsoever.

There is not the slightest necessity for doing so. Indeed, any attempt to use your will upon others will only tend to defeat your purpose.

You do not need to apply your will to things in order to compel them to come to you. That would simply be trying to coerce God and would be foolish and useless, as well as irreverent.

You do not have to compel God to give you good things any more than you have to use your will power to make the sun rise.

You do not have to use your will power to conquer an unfriendly deity, or to make stubborn and rebellious forces do your bidding.

The formless substance is friendly to you and is more willing to give you what you want than you are to get it. To get rich, you need only to use your will power upon yourself.

When you know what to think and do, then you must use your will to compel and discipline yourself to think and do the right things. That is the legitimate use of the will in getting what you want; that is, to use it in holding yourself to the right course.

Use your will to keep yourself thinking and acting in the certain way.

Do not try to project your will, your thoughts, or your mind out into space or to act upon things or people.

Keep your mind at home. It can accomplish more there than elsewhere.

Use your mind to form a mental image of what you want and to hold that vision with faith and purpose. Use your will to keep your mind working in the right way.

The more steady and continuous your faith and purpose, the more rapidly you will get rich, because you will make only positive impressions and thoughts upon the formless substance and you will not neutralize or offset them by negative impressions and thoughts.

The mental picture of your desires held with faith and purpose is taken up by the formless substance and permeates it to great distances - perhaps even throughout the entire universe.

As this impression spreads, all things are set moving toward its realization.

Every living thing, every inanimate thing, and the things yet uncreated, are stirred toward bringing into being that which you want. All force begins to be exerted in that direction and all things begin to move toward you.

You can check all this by starting a negative impression or thought in the formless substance. Doubt or unbelief is as certain to start a movement away from you as faith and purpose are to start one toward you.

It is by not understanding this that most people who try to make use of "mental science" in getting rich make their failure.

Every hour and moment you spend in giving heed to doubts and fears, every hour you spend in worry, every hour in which your soul is possessed by unbelief sets a current away from you in the whole domain of the intelligent substance.

Since belief is all important, it seriously benefits you to guard your thoughts. As your beliefs will be shaped to a very great extent by the things you observe and think about, it is important that you should command and focus your attention.

RJR: There are a myriad of things that we all have the choice to place our focus upon these days. Never before in human history have we all been more connected to one another - and there are truly amazing and wonderful things happening all over the world.

At the same time, the mainstream and corporate news media (on both sides of the political spectrum) will often only focus on the sensational, the violent, the fearful, and the dramatic things that are going on because that is how they make their money.

It does not have to be this way. *It has perhaps never been more important to learn how to be very intentional and selective in what you feed your mind upon - because what you feed your mind upon will ultimately determine the worldview that you adopt and how you conduct yourself.*

It has often been said "you are what you think" - so choose carefully.

Here the will comes into use, for it is by your will that you determine upon what things your attention shall be fixed.

If you want to become rich, you must not make a study of poverty.

Things are not brought into being by thinking about their opposites. Health is never to be attained by studying disease and thinking about disease.

Righteousness is not to be promoted by studying sin and thinking about sin.

...and no one ever got rich by studying poverty and thinking about poverty.

Medicine as a science of disease has increased disease; religion as a science of sin has promoted sin, and economics as a study of poverty will fill the world with wretchedness and want.

Do not talk about poverty. Do not investigate it or concern yourself with it. Never mind what its causes are, as you have nothing to do with them.

What concerns you is the cure.

Do not spend your time in typical charitable work, or typical charity movements. Most typical charity work only tends to perpetuate the wretchedness it aims to eradicate.

I do not say that you should be hard hearted or unkind and refuse to hear the cry of need...but you must not try to eradicate poverty in any of the conventional ways. Put poverty behind you, and put all that pertains to it behind you. **Focus on creating the good.**

Get rich - that is the best way that you can help the poor.

You cannot hold to the mental image which will make you rich if you fill your mind with pictures of poverty.

Do not focus on books, articles or papers which give circumstantial accounts of the wretchedness of the tenement dwellers, of the horrors of child labor, and so on.

Do not read anything which fills your mind with gloomy images of want and suffering.

You cannot help the poor in the least by focusing upon all of these things. The wide-spread knowledge of them does not tend at all to do away with poverty.

What tends to do away with poverty is not the getting of pictures of poverty into your mind, but getting pictures of wealth into the minds of the poor.

You are not deserting the poor in their misery when you refuse to allow your mind to be filled with pictures of that misery.

Poverty can be done away with - not by increasing the number of well to do people who think and focus on poverty - but by increasing the number of poor people who purpose with faith to get rich and rise out of poverty.

The poor do not need charity - they need inspiration. A lot of charity only sends them a loaf of bread to keep them alive in their poverty or gives them entertainment to make them forget for an hour or two.

Inspiration will cause them to want to rise out of their misery.

If you want to help the poor, demonstrate to them that they can become rich. You can prove it by getting rich yourself.

The only way in which poverty will ever be banished from this world is by getting a large and constantly increasing number of people to learn how to create wealth for themselves and their loved ones by the creative method.

People must be taught to become rich by creation, not by competition.

Every person who becomes rich by competition throws down behind them the ladder by which they rose and keeps others down.

On the contrary, every person who gets rich by the creative method opens a way for thousands to follow them and inspires many to do so.

You are not showing hardness of heart or an unfeeling disposition when you refuse to pity poverty, focus on poverty, read about poverty, think or talk about it, or to listen to those who do talk endlessly about it.

Use your will power to keep your mind OFF the subject of poverty, and to keep it fixed with faith and purpose ON the vision of what you want and the creative method of getting rich.

__RJR:__ This is not to say that there aren't amazing charities and people all over the world doing great work for those in need. What Wattles is saying is that unless you plan to go into that kind of work, the best thing you can do is make sure that your own household is well taken care of before you go about trying to help so many others.

__Again, this is an issue of "loving your neighbor as you love yourself"__ - you must love yourself first. Think of it in the same way that you must first put your own oxygen mask on during an in-flight emergency before you can help someone else. By filling your mind with possibility, inspiration, hope, and the faith and demonstration that you can rise out of your own financial troubles, you pave the way for countless others who will see your example.

If you truly desire to get involved in working with or starting a non-profit or a charity to help out those that are in need, good! My encouragement to you would be to do so in a way that empowers and educates those whom you help in harnessing the creative process and a lot of the topics mentioned in this book if you are truly interested in helping people out of poverty.

(If that is something that appeals to you, connect with me at https://www.ScienceOfGettingRich.info and we can chat about sending copies of this book to you in bulk if you so desire.)

Also, do not take from this chapter that Wattles is suggesting you should 'stick your head in the sand' about real issues and important events going on in your world and your community. What I believe he is saying is to get a healthy dose of perspective when it comes to the prevailing worldview that you adhere to.

Put simply, if you believe the world is falling apart, you will act accordingly, even if that is not actually true.

On the flip side, if you focus on the good, the true, the peaceful, the encouraging, and the hopeful things in your world, your mood will be better, your actions will be much more positive, and you can focus more on creating a better world for you and your loved ones.

Henry Ford famously said, "Whether you think you can, or think you can't, you're right." This is coming from a guy who disrupted the entire horse and buggy method of transportation with his automobiles! He likely would not have done all the things that he did if he believed that the world was ending like many even in his day were saying.

The doomsday prophets and sensationalist fearmongers have always been around - and likely always will be. They prey on people's fear to enrich themselves. The number of times they have been wrong with their end-of-the-world or terrible predictions has far exceeded any times they were right.

Prove them wrong again. **Create something better.**

Get your own financial troubles sorted out - get rich by the creative method - and empower others to do the same. *We are all in this thing together.*

As mentioned earlier, Lynn Twist's book "The Soul of Money" addresses this topic in great detail and I highly recommend it along with the other books mentioned at the back of this book.

**DON'T FIND FAULT.
FIND A REMEDY.**

- Henry Ford -

CHAPTER 10: FURTHER USE OF THE WILL

You cannot retain a true and clear vision of wealth if you are constantly turning your attention to opposing pictures, whether they be external or imaginary.

Do not tell of your past troubles of a financial nature. If you have had them, do not think of them at all.

Do not tell of the poverty of your parents or the hardships of your early life. To do any of these things is to mentally class yourself with the poor for the time being, and it will certainly slow the movement of things in your direction.

"Let the dead bury their dead," as Jesus said.

Put poverty and all things that pertain to poverty completely behind you.

You have accepted a certain theory of the universe as being correct, and are resting all your hopes of happiness on its being correct. What can you gain by giving heed to conflicting theories?

Do not read religious books which tell you that the world is soon coming to an end, and do not read the writing of muck-rakers, naysayers, and pessimistic philosophers who tell you that the world is going to the devil.

The world is not going to the devil, it is going to God. It is wonderful becoming.

RJR: *Regardless of your personal religious beliefs, let's talk about the concept of 'faith' for a moment. Either you choose to have faith, believe in, and focus on the things that are getting better in this world or you choose to have faith, believe in, and focus on the things that are getting worse. Your choice here will ultimately define the kind of life that you live and the results you see. If you believe the world is collapsing, you'll act like it and likely, your world will seem like it is collapsing.*

However, if that story you've been telling yourself isn't working out for you, what would it look like to tell yourself a different story for a change?

True, there may be a good many things in existing conditions which are disagreeable and upsetting, but what is the use of studying them when they are certainly passing away and when the study of them only tends to delay their passing and keep them with us?

Why give time and attention to things which are being removed by evolutionary growth when you can hasten their removal only by speeding up that evolutionary growth as far as your part of it goes?

No matter how horrible conditions in certain countries, sections, or places seem to be, you waste your time and destroy your own chances by focusing on them.

You should interest yourself in the world's becoming rich. Think of the riches the world is coming into instead of the poverty it is growing out of.

Bear in mind that the only way in which you can assist the world in growing rich is by growing rich yourself through the creative method, not the competitive one.

Give your attention wholly to riches and do not focus on poverty.

Whenever you think or speak of those who are poor, think and speak of them as those who are becoming rich - as those who are to be empowered rather than pitied. Then they and others will catch the inspiration, and begin to search for the way out.

RJR: *As mentioned elsewhere, this is not to imply that working in organizations that actually and practically help the poor is frowned upon - but bear in mind that it does no one any good to leave them in their poverty. Educate and empower them out of it.*

Because I say that you are to give your whole time and mind and thought to riches, it does not follow that you are to be cruel or mean.

To become really rich is the noblest aim you can have in life, for it includes everything else. On the competitive plane, the struggle to get rich is a Godless scramble for power over other people, but when we come into the creative mind, all this is changed.

All that is possible in the way of greatness, soul unfoldment, service and lofty endeavor comes by way of getting rich. All is made possible by the use of things.

If you lack for physical health, you will find that the attainment of it is conditional on your getting rich.

Only those who are emancipated from financial worry and who have the means to live a care-free existence and follow hygienic practices can have and retain health.

Moral and spiritual greatness is possible only to those who rise above the competitive battle for existence. Only those who are becoming rich on the plane of creative thought are free from the degrading influences of competition.

RJR: *If you think about this for a moment, you will find that it is true. Especially if you have ever (or have long been) in financial circumstances that have you worried about whether or not you are going to be able to keep food on the table. It is **very** difficult to think about anything else if you aren't sure that your basic needs will be met. That is the gist of what Wattles is getting at here. Without your physical, emotional, and financial needs taken care of, it becomes very hard to function at all.*

Whether we like it or not, having an abundance of finances to handle the issues of life makes dealing with them much simpler. At least the way I've come to look at things over the years, it is better to focus on acknowledging this fact and get on with the work of making it happen instead of getting into fruitless debates about whether or not "getting rich" is a good idea.

The idea that there is more than enough for everyone can be hard to comprehend when we have all been so conditioned to function from a mentality of lack versus a mentality of abundance. **Choose to believe it.**

If your heart is set on domestic happiness, remember that love flourishes best where there is refinement, a high level of thought, and freedom from corrupting influences. These are to be found only where riches are attained by the exercise of creative thought, without strife or rivalry.

I repeat, you can aim at nothing so great or noble as to become rich. You must fix your attention upon your mental picture of riches to the exclusion of all thoughts or theories that may tend to dim or obscure that vision.

You must learn to see the underlying truth in all things. You must see beneath all seemingly wrong conditions that there is the great one life ever moving forward toward fuller expression and more complete happiness.

It is the truth that there is no such thing as poverty - there is only wealth.

RJR: *I believe the key to not getting tripped up on this section is in recognizing that Wattles is drawing our attention to the fact that there is a wealth of abundant resources and solutions to problems all over the planet. When we embrace the creative process over the competitive one, we will find ways to work together and tap into the riches and resources that are all around us. Can you imagine what would happen if the fossil fuel industry would work more WITH those who are trying to create a cleaner, sustainable future of energy instead of trying to keep things the way they have been for so long?*

Some people remain in poverty because they are ignorant of the fact that there is wealth for them. These people can best be taught by showing them the way to affluence in your own person and practice.

Some are poor because while they feel that there is a way out, they are too intellectually lazy to put forth the mental effort necessary to find that way and travel by it. For these, the very best thing you can do is to arouse their desire by showing them the happiness that comes from getting rich via the creative method, not the competitive one.

Others still are poor because, while they have some notion of science, they have become so swamped and lost in the maze of metaphysical and occult theories that they do not know which road to take. They try a mixture of many systems and fail in all. For these, again, the best thing to do is to show the right way in your own person and practice.

An ounce of doing things is worth a pound of theorizing.

The very best thing you can do for the whole world is to make the most of yourself.

You can serve God and humanity in no more effective way than by getting rich. *That is, if you get rich by the creative method and not by the competitive one.*

I assert that this book gives in detail the principles of the science of getting rich. If that is true, you do not need to read any other book upon the subject. This may sound narrow and egotistical, but consider that there is no more scientific method of computation in mathematics than by addition, subtraction, multiplication, and division; no other method is possible.

There can be but one shortest distance between two points. There is only one way to think scientifically, and that is to think in the way that leads by the most direct and simple route to the goal. No one has yet formulated a briefer or less complex "system" than the one set forth in this book. It has been stripped of all non-essentials.

When you begin doing this, lay all others aside - put them out of your mind altogether. Read this book every day; keep it with you; commit it to memory, and do not think about other "systems" and theories. If you do, you may begin to have doubts and to be uncertain and wavering in your thoughts and actions, and then you will begin to make failures.

After you have made good and become rich, you may study other systems as much as you please; but until you are quite sure that you have gained what you want, do not read anything on this subject but this book.

RJR: *As I have stated elsewhere, I am not so dogmatic about this as Wattles was. My biggest encouragement with anything that you read or any information that you consume is to "eat the meat and spit out the bones," as it were. Test everything with your own experiences and don't just believe things because some authority figure told you to.*

The point of "science" of any kind is to test it out and see what works for you in practice, right?

Don't get so caught up on some of the overly confident sections of this book when Wattles talks in that way - focus instead of how to tap into your own creativity and learn ways to bring your own value into the marketplace.

Read only the most optimistic comments on the world's news - those in harmony with your mental picture.

Also, postpone your investigations into the occult. Do not dabble in theosophy, spiritualism, or kindred studies. It is very likely that the dead still live and are near - but if they are, let them alone. Mind your own business.

Wherever the spirits of the dead may be, they have their own work to do, and their own problems to solve. We have no right to interfere with them. We cannot help them, and it is very doubtful whether they can help us, or whether we have any right to trespass upon their time if they can.

Let the dead and the hereafter alone, and solve your own problems: get rich.

If you begin to mix with the occult, you will start mental cross-currents which will likely bring your hopes to shipwreck.

RJR: *So many of us can get easily caught up in arguing about religion, dogma, and our beliefs about what happens after this life.*

The fact is that none of us know for sure and it is fruitless to debate about these things. *I have found that life is much more peaceful when I leave these matters to each individual instead of feeling like it is my responsibility to save anyone or tell anyone else what to believe.*

So many of us grew up with a wide variety of beliefs about money, politics, and religion, and most of it just leads to arguments when we insist that we are right. Focus on what you can be sure of and what you can create.

Now, this and the preceding chapters have brought us to the following statement of basic facts:

- There is a thinking stuff from which all things are made, and which, in its original state, permeates, penetrates, and fills the interspaces of the universe.

- A thought in this substance produces the thing that is imagined by the thought.

- Humanity can form things in their thoughts, and by impressing their thoughts upon formless substance can cause the things they think about to be created.

- In order to do this, humanity must pass from the competitive to the creative mind.

- You must form a clear mental picture of the things you want. Hold this picture in your thoughts with the fixed purpose to get what you want and the unwavering faith that you will get what you want, closing your mind against all that may tend to shake your purpose, dim your vision, or quench your faith.

In addition to all of this, we shall now see that you must live and **act** in a certain way.

I AM CONVINCED ALL OF HUMANITY IS BORN WITH MORE GIFTS THAN WE KNOW. MOST ARE BORN GENIUSES AND JUST GET DE-GENIUSED RAPIDLY.

- Buckminster Fuller -

CHAPTER 11: ACTING IN THE CERTAIN WAY

Thought is the creative power or the impelling force which causes the creative power to act. Thinking in a certain way will bring riches to you, but you must not rely upon thought alone, paying no attention to personal action.

That is the rock upon which many otherwise scientific metaphysical thinkers meet shipwreck - *the failure to connect thought with personal action.*

We have not yet reached the stage of development, (even supposing such a stage to be possible), in which humanity can create directly from the formless substance without nature's processes or the work of human hands.

You must not only think, but your personal action must supplement your thought.

By thought you can cause the gold in the hearts of the mountains to be impelled toward you, but it will not mine itself, refine itself, coin itself into double eagles, and come rolling along the roads seeking its way into your pocket.

Under the impelling power of the supreme spirit, humanity's affairs will be so ordered that someone will be led to mine the gold for you, other people's business transactions will be so directed that the gold will be brought toward you, and you must so arrange your own business affairs that you may be able to receive it when it comes to you.

Your thought makes all things, animate and inanimate, work to bring you what you want...but your personal activity must be such that you can rightly receive what you want when it reaches you.

You are not to take it as charity, nor to steal it - you must give every person more in use value than they give you in cash value.

The scientific use of thought consists in forming a clear and distinct mental image of what you want...in holding fast to the purpose to get what you want, and in realizing with grateful faith that you will get what you want.

Do not try to 'project' your thought in any mysterious or occult way, with the idea of having it go out and do things for you. That is wasted effort and will weaken your power to think with sanity.

The action of thought in getting rich is fully explained in the preceding chapters.

Your faith and purpose positively impresses your vision upon the formless substance, which has the same desire for more life that you have. This vision, received from you, sets all the creative forces at work in and through their regular channels of action, but directed toward you.

It is not your part to guide or supervise the creative process - all you have to do with that is retain your vision, stick to your purpose, and maintain your faith and gratitude.

You must act in a certain way so that you can steward what is yours when it comes to you and so that you can receive the things you have in your mental picture and put them in their proper places as they arrive.

RJR: A quick note on this bit about you having no part in guiding or supervising the creative process...I believe what he is talking about is that it is not your responsibility to try and force something to happen that is largely the responsibility of someone else (as he mentioned not trying to 'project' your thoughts in a mysterious or occult way).

I DO believe it is your responsibility to do everything you can with what you have where you are in order to see the attaining of your goals and dreams. Plain and simple - "acting in the certain way" boils down to taking action on the vision that you have for yourself and the life that you desire.

That includes learning how to recognize your own value that you bring to the marketplace and figuring out ways to ensure that you are receiving what you are due for any creative work that you perform for someone else.

You can really see the truth of this. When things reach you, they will be in the hands of other people who will ask an equivalent for them. And you can only get what is yours by giving the other person what is his.

Your pocketbook is not going to be transformed magically into a limitless supply which will be always full of money without effort on your part.

This is the crucial point in the science of getting rich: right here, where thought and personal action must be combined.

There are very many people who (consciously or unconsciously) set the creative forces in action by the strength and persistence of their desires, but who remain poor because they do not provide for the reception of the thing they want when it comes.

***RJR:** By this, I believe that the author is referring to practical matters like setting up appropriate bank accounts (a business account, if you are going into business for yourself, for example), creating marketing plans for your product or service, implementing systems to help you work more efficiently, networking with business partners, etc.*

By thought, the thing you want is brought to you. It is by action that you receive it.

Whatever your action is to be, it is evident that you must act NOW. You cannot act in the past, and it is essential to the clearness of your mental vision that you dismiss the past from your mind.

You cannot act in the future, for the future is not here yet. And you cannot tell how you will want to act in any future contingency until that contingency has arrived.

Because you are not in the right business or the right environment now, do not think that you must postpone action until you get into the right business or environment.

Do not spend time in the present worrying about taking the best course in possible future emergencies: have faith in your ability to meet any emergency when it arrives.

If you act in the present with your mind on the future, your present action will be with a divided mind, and will not be effective.

Put your whole mind into present action.

Do not give your creative impulse to the original substance and then sit down and wait for results. If you do, you will never get them. Act now.

There is never any time but now, and there never will be any time but now. If you are ever to begin to make ready for the reception of what you want, you must begin now.

The action you take, whatever it is, must be in your present business or employment, and must be upon the persons and things in your present environment.

You cannot act where you are not. You cannot act where you have been, and you cannot act where you are going to be. You can act only where you are.

Do not bother as to whether yesterday's work was well done or not; do today's work well.

Do not try to do tomorrow's work now; there will be plenty of time to do that when you get to it.

Do not try by occult or mystical means to act on people or things that are out of your reach.

Do not wait for a change of environment before you act - get a change of environment by action. You can act upon the environment in which you are now to cause yourself to be transferred to a better environment.

RJR: You can create better situations for yourself right where you are that will ultimately lead to improved situations in the future. One of the things that I have found extremely helpful in cultivating a more creative, fulfilling life is to intentionally set up an environment that makes doing your creative work easy. The key is making it simple for you to "get in the zone."

***Want to be a better musician?** Set up your instrument in a more prominent location in your home and play it at least ten minutes a day.*

***Want to be a better writer?** Get a journal and write for at least ten minutes every morning when you wake up and for ten minutes just before you go to sleep.*

*Just ten minutes! What do you have to lose? So much of this "success" thing really boils down to one thing: **intentional self-discipline.***

Hold in mind with faith and purpose the vision of yourself in the better environment, but act upon your present environment with all your heart, with all your strength, and with all your mind.

Do not waste your time just day dreaming or castle building; hold to the one vision of what you want, and act NOW.

RJR: I don't know about you, but I can certainly attest to getting stuck here over the years! How many times have we been in unfavorable situations or environments and rather than taking practical action to DO something about getting out of them, we instead waste our time and energy wallowing in our misery, complaining to friends/co-workers/family members, and generally just staying stuck in our self-loathing?

As Robert Frost has said, "The best way out is always through." This is the part of the book that really kicked my butt into high gear - because it helped me to realize how much of my energy was being wasted wishing for something to change instead of actually doing something that would cause change to happen.

Do you hate your job? *Have you actually started looking for other work? Feeling frustrated with that client that seems to be more of a trouble to deal with than the money they pay you? Have you considered finding ways to let them go and make more money elsewhere for less hassle?*

Just some things to consider...

Do not cast about seeking some new thing to do or some strange, unusual, or remarkable action to perform as a first step toward getting rich. It is probable that your actions, at least for some time to come, will be those you have been performing for awhile. Realize that you are to begin now to perform these actions in the certain way which will surely make you rich.

If you are engaged in some kind of business and feel that it is not the right one for you, do not wait until you get into the right business before you begin to act.

Do not feel discouraged or sit down and lament because you are misplaced. No person was ever so misplaced that they could not find the right place, and no person ever became so involved in the wrong business that they could not get into the right business.

Hold the mental vision of yourself in the right business with the purpose and faith that you will get into it and are getting into it, but ACT in your present business and location.

Use your present business as the means of getting a better one, and use your present environment as the means of getting into a better one.

Your vision of the right business, if held with faith and purpose, will cause the supreme power to move the right business toward you. Your action, if performed in the certain way, will cause you to move toward that business.

If you are an employee or wage earner and feel that you must change places in order to get what you want, do not project your thought into space and rely upon it to get you another job. It will probably fail to do so.

Hold the vision of yourself in the job you want while you ACT with faith and purpose in the job you have and you will certainly get the job you want.

RJR: *(In a nutshell, if you hate your job, start applying for new ones ASAP or work on a side hustle and don't quit until you see it happen. Nobody ever said this was 'easy', just that it works.)*

Your vision and faith will set the creative force in motion to bring it toward you, and your action will cause the forces in your own environment to move you toward the place you want.

In closing this chapter, we will add another statement to our syllabus:

- There is a thinking stuff from which all things are made, and which, in its original state, permeates, penetrates, and fills the interspaces of the universe.

- A thought in this substance produces the thing that is imagined by the thought.

- Humanity can form things in their thoughts, and by impressing their thoughts upon formless substance can cause the things they think about to be created.

- In order to do this, humanity must pass from the competitive to the creative mind.

- You must form a clear mental picture of the things you want. Hold this picture in your thoughts with the fixed purpose to get what you want and the unwavering faith that you will get what you want, closing your mind against all that may tend to shake your purpose, dim your vision, or quench your faith.

- So that you may receive what you want when it comes, you must act **NOW** upon the people and things in your present environment.

LIFE SHRINKS OR EXPANDS IN PROPORTION TO ONE'S COURAGE.

- Anaïs Nin -

CHAPTER 12: EFFICIENT ACTION

You must use your thought as directed in previous chapters, and begin to do what you can do where you are, and you must do ALL that you can do where you are.

You can advance only by being larger than your present place and no person is larger than their present place who leaves undone any of the work pertaining to that place.

The world is advanced only by those who more than fill their present places.

If no person quite filled their present place, you can see that everything would start to regress backwards. Those who do not quite fill their present places are a weight upon society, government, commerce, and industry.

They must be carried along by others at a great expense. The progress of the world is hindered only by those who do not fill the places they are holding. They belong to a former age and a lower stage or plane of life, and their tendency is toward degeneration.

No society could advance if every person was smaller than their place. Social evolution is guided by the law of physical and mental evolution. In the animal world, evolution is caused by excess of life.

When an organism has more life than can be expressed in the functions of its own plane, it develops the organs of a higher plane, and a new species is originated.

There never would have been new species had there not been organisms which more than filled their places.

The law is exactly the same for you; your getting rich depends upon your applying this principle to your own affairs and business.

Every day is either a successful day or a day of failure, and it is the successful days which get you what you want. If everyday is a failure, you can never get rich. On the contrary, if every day is a success, you cannot fail to get rich.

If there is something that may be done today and you do not do it, you have failed in so far as that thing is concerned and the consequences may be more disastrous than you imagine.

You cannot foresee the results of even the most trivial act. You do not know the workings of all the forces that have been set moving on your behalf.

Much may be depending on your doing some simple act that may be the very thing which will open the door of opportunity to great possibilities and opportunities.

You can never know all the combinations which the supreme intelligence is making for you in the world of things and of human affairs.

Your neglect or failure to do some small thing today may cause a long delay in getting what you want.

Do, every day, ALL that can be done that day.

There is, however, a limitation or qualification of the above that you must take into account.

You are not to overwork, nor to rush blindly into your business in the effort to do the greatest possible number of things in the shortest possible time.

You are not to try to do tomorrow's work today, nor to do a week's work in a day.

It is really not the number of things you do, but the EFFICIENCY of each separate action that counts.

RJR: If you are not familiar with it already, do a web search for "the 80/20 principle". This is also known as the Pareto Principle and it states that about 80% of the results you get come from 20% of the actions you are taking.

For example, in sports training roughly 20% of certain exercises and habits have 80% of the impact in the athlete. Tim Ferriss often will use the phrase "the minimum effective dose" when discussing those actions that, if taken consistently over time, will produce the desired results much faster.

It requires a good bit of self-awareness to pay attention to how you are using your time and energy, but if you do an 80/20 analysis of your actions you should find relatively quickly where most of your results are coming from.

That is, if you are spending 80% of your 'free time' binging on Netflix or some other form of mindless entertainment/social media instead of building your creative skillset, chances are you won't achieve the results you want very quickly.

For our creative agency (http://www.reformdesigns.biz), approximately 80% of our income and opportunity comes from 20% of our clients. Many business owners will acknowledge this spread is fairly accurate for their own endeavors and pursuits.

Every act is, in itself, either a success or a failure. Every act is, in itself, either effective or inefficient. Every inefficient act is a failure, and if you spend your life doing inefficient acts, your whole life will be a failure.

The more things you do, the worse for you if all your acts are inefficient ones. On the other hand, every efficient act is a success in itself. If every act of your life is an efficient one, your whole life MUST be a success.

The cause of failure is doing too many things in an inefficient manner and not doing enough things in an efficient manner.

You will see that it is a self-evident proposition that if you do not do any inefficient acts but instead do a sufficient number of efficient acts, you will become rich. If it is possible for you to make each act an efficient one, you see again that the getting of riches is reduced to an exact science, like mathematics.

RJR: *If you have been an employee of someone else for the majority of your life up to this point, one of the most difficult battles you will face is learning how to be more self-directed in your goal-setting and income generation as opposed to having someone tell you what to do all day long.*

If you ever do want freedom from the 9-5 lifestyle, you should start figuring out how to better master and use your time and energy when you're not at work in the direction of pursuing what you really want...because once you don't have a boss to give you orders anymore, you're the boss now!

(If you'd like some help mastering your time better, check out https://www.stopwastingtime.today)

The matter turns, then, on the question of whether you can make each separate act a success in itself, and this you can certainly do. You can make each act a success because the supreme power is working with you and the supreme power cannot fail.

The supreme power is at your service. To make each act efficient you have only to put your own creativity and willpower into it.

Every action is either strong or weak. When every action is strong and focused, you are acting in the certain way which will make you rich.

Every act can be made strong and efficient by holding your vision while you are doing it, and putting the whole power of your FAITH and PURPOSE into it.

It is at this point that the people fail who separate mental power from personal action. They use the power of mind in one place and at one time and they act in another place and at another time. Their acts are not successful in themselves and too many of them are inefficient.

RJR: *I've heard this called "mental time travel". Think about it - how much of your mental energy is wasted worrying about the future, regretting the past, and ignoring the present moment? Not only are none of these mental gymnastics completely useless, but they also slow you down immensely from the attainment of the goals which you seek.*

If you find yourself mentally time traveling, slow down - take a few deep breaths - now repeat to yourself, "This is not useful" - and move on. *(Thanks to James Altucher for this tip.)*

The only way you will accomplish that which you seek to accomplish is by putting your energy and focus on the present moment and acting accordingly.

If you welcome the supreme creative power into every act no matter how commonplace, every act will be a success in itself. As in the nature of things, every success opens the way to other successes.

In this way, your progress towards what you want and the progress of what you want coming towards you will become increasingly rapid.

Remember that successful action is cumulative in its results. Since the desire for more life is inherent in all things, when you begin to move toward larger life, more things attach themselves to you, and the influence of your desire is multiplied.

RJR: *In general, people want to be around others that they perceive are "going somewhere". Very rarely will you see a person who does not have the outward appearance of "success" amassing large numbers of followers around them.*

This is not to say that financial success is the only type of success - but it is to draw your attention to the fact that overall, if you give off the appearance (and of course, demonstrate) that you are "going somewhere" with your life, naturally people and opportunity will gravitate more towards you.

Do every day all that you can do that day and do each act in an efficient manner.

In saying that you must hold your vision while you are doing each act, however trivial or commonplace, I do not mean to say that it is necessary at all times to see the vision distinctly to its smallest details. It should be the work of your leisure hours to use your imagination on the details of your vision and to contemplate them until they are firmly fixed in your mind.

If you wish speedy results, use as much time as you can in this practice of intentional meditation, then take action.

RJR: *You can do this in practical ways by adding to your vision board, visiting new places that inspire you, and spending time with people who champion you and your goals.*

Do not waste your time and energy hanging around people who just drag you down or in consuming information that just leaves you fearful and hopeless. It will not help you achieve your goals and will surely delay you in reaching them.

By continuous contemplation, you will get the picture of what you want, down even to the smallest details firmly fixed upon your mind. This will be transferred to the mind of the formless substance. In your working hours, you need only to mentally refer to the picture to stimulate your faith and purpose, and cause your best effort to be put forth.

Contemplate your picture in your leisure hours until your consciousness is so full of it that you can grasp it instantly. You will become so enthused with its bright promises that the mere thought of it will call forth the strongest energies of your whole being.

RJR: *Another note here on the "formless substance" term - perhaps another way to look at it is to consider it to be like your subconscious. What you focus on and think about will grow in your mind, etc. You can also 'contemplate your picture' by looking regularly at your notes, your vision boards, and things you hang up around your home or office to keep you inspired and focused.*

...and if you are looking for some inspirational wall decor, make sure to check out https://www.RDShop.biz

Let us again repeat our syllabus, and by slightly changing the closing statements bring it to the point we have now reached.

- There is a thinking stuff from which all things are made, and which, in its original state, permeates, penetrates, and fills the interspaces of the universe.

- A thought in this substance produces the thing that is imagined by the thought.

- Humanity can form things in their thoughts, and by impressing their thoughts upon formless substance can cause the things they think about to be created.

- In order to do this, humanity must pass from the competitive to the creative mind.

- You must form a clear mental picture of the things you want, and do, with faith and purpose, all that can be done each day to achieve that goal, doing each separate thing in an efficient manner.

- You must act **NOW** upon the people and things in your present environment.

IT IS NOT THE MOUNTAIN THAT WE CONQUER, BUT OURSELVES.

- Edmund Hillary -

CHAPTER 13: GETTING INTO THE RIGHT BUSINESS

Success, in any particular business, depends for one thing upon your possessing in a well-developed state the faculties and skills required in that business.

Without good musical faculty, no one can succeed as a teacher of music. Without well-developed mechanical faculties, no one can achieve great success in any of the mechanical trades. Without tact and the commercial faculties, no one can succeed in mercantile and business pursuits.

RJR:** A quick note here - don't think for a moment that if you desire to learn how to do something but don't feel "gifted" at it that you cannot teach yourself how to do whatever that thing is. **No musician started out being an amazing musician. No artist ever started out being a world-class artist. It all takes practice - lots, and lots, and lots of practice.

If you want to do something and don't know how to do it, put in the work and learn. Don't wait around for creativity to just magically bestow these gifts upon you. It is work and practice over time that brings excellence. It is not luck or inherent talent. I have included additional resources & recommended reading at the end of this book to aid you in your learning and help you in your journey. You can learn just about anything for FREE.

Merely possessing the skills required in your particular vocation does not ensure getting rich. There are musicians who have remarkable talent and who yet remain poor. There are blacksmiths, carpenters, and so on who have excellent mechanical ability but who do not get rich. There are merchants with good faculties for dealing with people who nevertheless fail.

The different faculties are tools. It is essential to have good tools, but it is also essential that the tools should be used in the right way.

One person can take a sharp saw, a square, a good plane, and so on and build a handsome article of furniture. Another person can take the same tools and get to work to duplicate the article, but their production will be a botch.

Why? That person does not know how to use good tools in a successful way.

The various faculties of your mind are the tools with which you must do the work which will make you rich. It will be easier for you to succeed if you get into a business for which you are well equipped with the right mental tools.

Generally speaking, you will do best in that business which will use your strongest skills, these being the ones for which you are naturally "best fitted." But there are limitations to this statement, also. No one should regard their vocation as being irrevocably fixed by the tendencies or gifts with which they were born.

You can get rich in ANY business, for if you do not have the right talent for your particular desired business, you can develop and improve that talent.

It merely means that you will have to learn or make your tools as you go along, instead of confining yourself to the use of those with which you were born or which are presently available.

RJR: *Stated simply again: you can learn anything you want to...and especially these days, you can learn almost anything pretty much for free with the internet or in your local library. Don't believe the nonsense that you can't learn something new. You must simply cultivate the willpower to do so and put in the time and energy to do it. It's not glamorous, but it works!*

It will be EASIER for you to succeed in a vocation for which you already have the talents in a well-developed state, but you CAN succeed in any vocation, for you can develop any rudimentary talent, and there is no talent of which you have not at least a little of.

You will get rich most easily if you do that for which you are best fitted, but you will get rich most satisfactorily if you do that which you WANT to do.

Doing what you want to do is life. There is no real satisfaction in living if we are compelled to be forever doing something which we do not like to do and can never do what we want to do.

It is certain that you can do what you want to do - the desire to do it is proof that you have within you the power to do it.

Desire is a manifestation of power.

The desire to play music is the power which can play music seeking expression and development. The desire to invent mechanical devices is the mechanical talent seeking expression and development.

Where there is no power to do a thing, either developed or undeveloped, there is never any desire to do that thing. Where there is strong desire to do a thing, it is certain proof that the power to do it is strong, and only requires to be developed and applied in the right way.

All things otherwise being equal, it is best to select the business for which you have the best developed talent.

However, if you have a strong desire to engage in any particular line of work, you should select that work as your main goal.

You can do what you want to do, and because of that, it is your right and privilege to pursue the business or vocation which will be most desirable and pleasant.

You are not obliged to do what you do not like to do, and should not do it except as a means to bring you to the doing of the thing you want to do.

RJR: *In other words, don't believe that you're obligated to stay in a job you hate just because you feel like it's all that is available to you. You're better than that and there's plenty of opportunity out there. It will take work, effort, trial and error to get where you want to go, but you can do it if you put your mind to it and commit to the journey and your goals.*

If there are past mistakes whose consequences have placed you in an undesirable business or environment, you may be obliged for some time to do what you do not like to do, but you can make the doing of it pleasant by knowing that it is making it possible for you to come to the doing of what you want to do.

RJR: *Look at each place of work as a stepping stone to help you reach your next place of work until you reach the goals that you have for yourself. At the same time, do not tolerate abusive and disrespectful behavior by your superiors just to hold down a job. It isn't worth it. Leverage your network of friends, family, and fans and ask for help finding the kinds of opportunities that you seek. People are much more willing to help than most people are to ask. What do you have to lose? Your crappy job?*

If you feel that you are not in the right vocation, do not act too hastily in trying to get into another one. Generally, the best way to change your business or environment is by growth.

Do not be afraid to make a sudden and radical change if the opportunity is presented and you feel after careful consideration that it is the right opportunity. However, **never take sudden or radical action when you are in doubt as to the wisdom of doing so and lacking internal peace.**

There is never any hurry on the creative plane, and there is no lack of opportunity.

When you get out of the competitive mind, you will understand that you never need to act hastily. No one else is going to beat you to the thing you want to do. There is enough for all.

If one space is taken, another and a better one will be opened for you a little farther on. There is plenty of time. **When you are in doubt, wait.**

Fall back on the contemplation of your vision and increase your faith and purpose...and by all means, **in times of doubt and indecision, cultivate gratitude.**

A day or two spent in contemplating the vision of what you want and in earnest thanksgiving that you are getting it will bring your mind into such close relationship with the supreme power that you will make no mistake when you do act.

There is a mind which knows all there is to know, and you can come into close unity with this mind by faith and the purpose to advance in life if you have deep gratitude.

Mistakes come from acting hastily, from acting in fear or doubt, or in forgetfulness of the right motive - which is more life to all and less to none.

As you go on in the certain way, opportunities will come to you in increasing number. You will need to be very steady in your faith and purpose, and to keep in close touch with the infinite by reverent gratitude.

Do all that you can do in a perfect manner every day, but do it without haste, worry, or fear.

Go as fast as you can, but never hurry.

Remember that in the moment you begin to hurry you cease to be a creator and become a competitor.

This is when you drop back upon the old plane again. Whenever you find yourself hurrying, slow down, fix your attention on the mental image of the thing you want, and begin to give thanks that you are getting it.

The exercise of GRATITUDE will never fail to strengthen your faith and renew your purpose.

WITHOUT A HUMBLE BUT REASONABLE CONFIDENCE IN YOUR OWN POWERS, YOU CANNOT BE SUCCESSFUL OR HAPPY.

- Norman Vincent Peale -

CHAPTER 14: THE IMPRESSION OF INCREASE

Whether you change your vocation or not, your actions for the present must be those pertaining to the business in which you are now engaged.

You can get into the business you want by making constructive use of the business you are already established in by doing your daily work in a certain way.

As much as your business consists in dealing with other people, whether in person, by letter, or on the phone, the main thought of all your efforts must be to *convey to their minds the impression of increase.*

Increase is what all people are seeking.

It is the urge of the formless intelligence within them seeking fuller expression.

The desire for increase is inherent in all of nature. It is the fundamental impulse of the universe.

All human activities are based on the desire for increase. People are seeking more food, more clothes, better shelter, more luxury, more beauty, more knowledge, more pleasure -some kind of increase and more life.

Every living thing is operating with this necessity for continuous advancement. Where increase of life ceases, dissolution and death set in at once.

Humanity instinctively knows this, and hence we are forever seeking more. This law of perpetual increase is set forth by Jesus in the parable of the talents: only those who gain more retain any - and "from him who has not shall be taken away even that which he has."

The normal desire for increased wealth is not an evil or a reprehensible thing - it is simply the desire for more abundant life. It is aspiration.

Because it is the deepest instinct of their natures, all men and women are attracted to those who can give them more of the means of life.

In following the certain way as described in the previous pages, you are getting continuous increase for yourself and you are giving it to all with whom you deal.

You are a creative center from which increase is given off to all.

Be sure of this and convey assurance of that fact to every man, woman, and child with whom you come in contact. No matter how small the transaction, even if it be only the selling of a stick of candy to a little child, put into it the thought of increase, and make sure that the customer receives that impression. Show them this increase in action.

Convey the impression of advancement with everything you do so that all people shall receive the impression that you are an advancing person and that you advance all who deal with you.

Even to the people whom you meet in a social way *(without any thought of business and to whom you do not try to sell anything)*, give them the impression and thought of increase.

You can convey this impression by holding the unshakable faith that you, yourself, are in the way of increase and by letting this faith inspire, fill, and permeate every action.

Do everything that you do with the firm conviction that you are an advancing personality, and that you are giving advancement to everybody.

Feel that you are getting rich, and that in so doing you are making others rich, and conferring those benefits on everyone.

Do not boast or brag of your success or talk about it unnecessarily. True faith is never boastful.

Wherever you find a boastful person, you find one who is secretly doubtful and afraid.

Simply choose to feel faith and gratitude and let it work out in every transaction. Let every action, tone and look express the quiet assurance that you are getting rich and even that you are already rich.

Words will not be necessary to communicate this feeling to others. They will feel the sense of increase when in your presence and will be attracted to you again.

RJR: This can feel very difficult - especially if you are in a financial situation that seems on the surface to be the polar opposite of what you would consider "rich". Remember the bit about gratitude though - when you are feeling low and frustrated, step back from your bank account, walk away from all the unpaid bills, and take stock of what you DO have.

Be intentionally thankful for what you have right where you are - even if that is as simple as a roof over your head, food to eat, and the breath in your lungs. There are plenty of people around the world who struggle with even those basic needs.

"Being rich", as we have discussed throughout the book so far, is only partially a financial thing.

A much bigger part of it is the mindset that you adopt along the way. Don't let the consumerism of our age distract you from your blessings.

Your goal is to impress upon others that in associating with you, they will get increase for themselves. **See that you give them a use value greater than the cash value you are taking from them.**

Take an honest pride in doing this and let everybody know it. You will have no lack of customers. People will go where they are given increase. The supreme power which desires increase in all and which knows all will move toward you people who have never heard of you.

Your business will increase rapidly, and you will be surprised at the unexpected benefits which will come to you. You will be able from day to day to make larger connections, secure greater advantages, and to go on into a more pleasant vocation if you desire to do so.

However, in doing all this you must never lose sight of your vision of what you want and your faith and purpose to get what you want.

Let me here give you another word of caution in regard to motives:

Beware of the insidious temptation to seek for power over other people.

Nothing is so pleasant to the unformed or partially developed mind as the exercise of power or dominion over others.

The desire to rule for selfish gratification has been the curse of the world.

For countless ages, kings and lords have drenched the earth with blood in their battles to extend their dominions...not to seek more life for all, but to get more power for themselves.

Today, the primary motive in the business and industrial world is the same. People marshal their armies of dollars and lay waste the lives and hearts of millions in the same mad scramble for power over others. Commercial kings, like political kings, are often inspired by the lust for power.

Jesus saw in this desire for mastery over others the moving impulse of that evil world he sought to overthrow. Read the twenty-third chapter of

Matthew and see how he pictures the desire of the Pharisees to be called "Master," to sit in the high places, to domineer over others, and to lay burdens on the backs of the less fortunate. Note how he contrasts this lust for dominion with the brotherly seeking of the common good to which he calls his disciples.

Look out for the temptation to seek authority, to become a "master," to be considered as one who is above the common herd, to impress others by lavish display, and so on.

The mind that seeks for mastery over others is the competitive mind, and the competitive mind is not the creative one.

In order to master your environment and your destiny, it is not at all necessary that you should rule over anyone. Indeed, when you fall into the world's struggle for the high places, you begin to be conquered by fate and environment, and your getting rich becomes a matter of chance and speculation.

Beware of the competitive mind!

No better statement of the principle of creative action can be formulated than the favorite declaration of the late "Golden Rule" Jones:

"What I want for myself, I want for everybody."

RJR: I believe this chapter is one of the most important for anyone who is seeking to better themselves personally, professionally, and financially. It doesn't take a rocket scientist to figure out that what Wattles is saying here is spot on. Just think about what happens when those in positions of authority use their authority to manipulate, control, or domineer over others.

On the journey of life that we all are on, adopting the "golden rule" is something that pretty much everyone from every religion and political affiliation can (or at least in my opinion, should) agree on.

If they don't, they probably shouldn't be in a position of power. If they are, they likely are operating from the competitive mind which only creates problems and conflict over time.

We can all do better if we choose to.

The key is keeping the main thing the main thing and making sure that you aren't getting caught up in the fruitless pursuit of power for power's sake.

OTHER PEOPLE'S OPINION OF YOU DOES NOT HAVE TO BECOME YOUR REALITY.

- Les Brown -

CHAPTER 15: THE ADVANCING PERSON

What I have said in the last chapter applies as much to the professional individual and the wage-earner/employee as it does to the one who is engaged in mercantile business.

No matter what you do for a living, whether you are a physician, a teacher, a pastor, or otherwise, if you can give increase of life to others and make them sensible of the fact, they will be attracted to you and you will get rich.

The physician who holds the vision of themselves as a great and successful healer and who works toward the complete realization of that vision with faith and purpose as described in former chapters will come into such close touch with the source of life that they will be phenomenally successful. Patients will come to them in throngs.

No one has a greater opportunity to carry into effect the teaching of this book than the practitioner of the healing arts. It does not matter to which of the various schools you may belong, for the principle of healing is common to all of them and may be reached by all alike.

The advancing person in medicine who holds to a clear mental image of themselves as successful and who obeys the laws of faith, purpose, and gratitude will cure every curable case they undertake, no matter what remedies they may use.

RJR: Disclaimer - I am not a medical doctor! While I agree with a number of Wattles' principles on a variety of topics, do exercise caution with claims like the above. Nothing in this book is to be considered medical advice of any kind and please make sure that you go through all proper channels and necessary certifications required for your field of study/medicine before making certain claims. As always, consult a professional if you have legitimate medical concerns.

In the field of religion, the world cries out for leaders who can teach their hearers the true science of abundant life. The person who masters the details of the science of getting rich, together with the allied sciences of being well, of being great, of winning love, and who teaches these details from the pulpit will never lack for a congregation.

This is the "gospel" that the world needs. It will give increase of life, people will hear it gladly and will give abundant support to the person who brings it to them.

RJR: *Many of you reading this likely grew up in a church environment - and even if that is not the case, it is worth noting that the word "gospel" can be translated into "very good news". It is likely evident to most people reading this that a lot of what is heard in many churches these days is not exactly "good news".*

Regardless of what faith you adhere to (or if you don't adhere to any at all), consider that it is good news indeed to hear that anyone who wants to can learn the art and science of doing better for themselves and their loved ones. It starts with you choosing to do and be better today than you were yesterday and recognizing that we're all in this together.

Don't get caught up in the noise of thinking this is "just some prosperity gospel nonsense." What Wattles is saying here is that what the world really needs is not to be beaten over the head with condemnation of how terrible they are. They don't need to be told that God is going to throw them in a volcano forever if they don't pray a prayer a certain way or go to a certain church three times a week, only read a certain translation of a religious text, or forget to say five Hail Mary's before bed.

What the world needs are tangible acts of love, life, grace, forgiveness, generosity, abundance, and the power to make a positive difference here and now - not just the promise of the possibility of a better afterlife.

What is now needed is a demonstration of the science of life from the pulpit. We want preachers who can not only tell us how, but who in their own lives will show us how. We need the preacher who will be rich, healthy, great, and beloved, to teach us how to attain these things. Those who do will find a numerous and loyal following.

The same is true of the teacher who can inspire the children with the faith and purpose of the advancing life. They will never be "out of a job."

Any teacher who has this faith and purpose can give it to their pupils. They cannot help giving it to them if it is part of their own life and practice.

What is true of the teacher, preacher, and physician is true of the lawyer, dentist, real estate and insurance agents. This is true of everybody.

The combined mental and personal action I have described is infallible; it cannot fail. Every man and woman who follows these instructions steadily, perseveringly, and to the letter, will get rich. The law of the increase of life is as mathematically certain in its operation as the law of gravitation. Getting rich is an exact science.

RJR: *Another obligatory disclaimer - I make no claims of this magnitude, as "getting rich" is always going to be a subjective term depending on your perspective.*

However, I will say that I have applied a number of the principles discussed in this book to my own life and have seen tangible results, increased earnings, influence, connections, etc.

Take that for what it's worth. I simply am not of the type that will so boldly say "this is the only way to do something" as Wattles does several times in the book...and I mention it repeatedly so you can't ever say I said otherwise :)

The wage-earner will find this as true of their case as of any of the others mentioned. Do not feel that you have no chance to get rich because you are working where there is no visible opportunity for advancement or where wages are small and the cost of living high.

Form your clear mental vision of what you want, and begin to act with faith and purpose.

Do all the work you can do every day, and do each piece of work in a perfectly successful and efficient manner. Put the power of success and the intention to get rich into everything that you do.

Do not do this merely with the idea of gaining favor with your employer in the hope that they or those above you will see your good work and advance you. It is not likely that they will do so.

The person who is merely a "good" employee filling their place to the very best of their ability (and is satisfied with that) is valuable to their employer.

It is not to the employer's interest to promote that person. To the employer, that employee is worth more where they are.

To secure advancement, something more is necessary than to be too large for your place.

The person who is certain to advance is the one who is too big for their place and who has a clear concept of what they want to be.

This person knows that they can become what they want to be and is determined to BE what they want to be.

Do not try to more than fill your present place with the intention of pleasing your employer. Do it with the idea of advancing yourself.

RJR: On this note - what Wattles is saying here is important. Don't think for a moment that if you suddenly start talking about how you're going to change your life, get rich, and live out all kinds of successful endeavors that your employer or fellow coworkers are going to take you seriously.

Chances are much higher that they will just think you are arrogant and won't want to be around you. Instead, do your work behind the scenes - whatever that may be. Write that book. Create that screenplay. Learn that instrument. Paint that painting.

Practice, practice, practice. *Over time, your skills will increase and opportunities will arise that will make it easier for you to transition out of your current position and into a place where you are doing more of the things that you'd like to be doing.*

Again, I repeat - do not boast about all the things you are doing and learning, ESPECIALLY in the workplace. If you are wanting to advance to a better position in your current job, that's fine - but keep in mind that the workplace can often be a very politically charged environment where most are in the competitive state of mind, not the creative one.

Rare is the standard workplace that places a high value on creativity and doesn't simply view "go-getters" as threats to the status quo. At least in my opinion (and experience), it's much better to let your work speak for itself over time. Austin Kleon's book "Show Your Work" is an excellent resource that expands on this topic.

Hold the faith and purpose of increase during work hours, after work hours, and before work hours. Hold it in such a way that every person who comes in contact with you - whether foreman, fellow employee, or social acquaintance - will feel the power of purpose radiating from you.

In this way, everyone will get the sense of advancement and increase from you. People will be attracted to you and if there is no possibility for advancement in your present job, you will very soon see an opportunity to take another job.

There is a power which never fails to present opportunity to the advancing person who is moving in obedience to universal laws.

God cannot help helping you if you act in a certain way. He must do so in order to help Himself.

There is nothing in your circumstances or in the industrial situation that can keep you down. If you cannot get rich working for a corporation, you can get rich in other ways.

If you begin to move in the certain way, you will certainly escape from the "clutches" of the corporations and get on to wherever else you wish to be.

If a few thousand of their employees would enter upon the creative and certain way, the corporations would soon be in a bad plight. They would have to give their employees more opportunity or go out of business.

Nobody has to work for less than what they are worth. You do not have to accept less than a living wage for the work that you do. Companies can keep people in so-called hopeless conditions only so long as there are people who are too ignorant to know of the science of getting rich or too intellectually slothful to practice it and do something about it.

***RJR:** Another quick note here - if you are in a situation where you are treated poorly by your employer, do yourself and your loved ones a favor and find a way out of that situation as soon as possible. The world is full of opportunities and you do not have to tolerate being treated unfairly, with disrespect, or paid low wages.*

The more that employees the world over realize that they are what makes their companies successful just as much as the people steering the ship, the sooner things will start changing en masse for the better.

Begin this way of thinking and acting and your faith and purpose will make you quick to see any opportunity to better your condition.

Such opportunities will speedily come, for the supreme power, working in all and working for you, will bring them before you.

Do not wait for an opportunity to be all that you want to be. When an opportunity to be more than you are now is presented and you feel impelled toward it, take it.

It will be the first step toward a greater opportunity.

It is impossible in this universe to lack opportunities for the person who is living the advancing life.

It is inherent in the constitution of the cosmos that all things shall be for you and work together for your good. The advancing person must certainly get rich if they act and think in the certain way.

Let wage-earning men and women study this book with great care, and enter with confidence upon the course of action it prescribes. It will not fail.

RJR: *You are capable of far more than you might currently believe. Apply yourself to learning new skills every day and bettering your existing skills and surely you will come across new opportunities that will be stepping stones to even bigger ones.*

Try not to think of "success" as something where you "get rich quick", but more like it is a journey that you are on.

Take it one step at a time, and choose to enjoy the ride.

It's not about arriving at some specific destination as much as it's about using what you've got where you are while you learn how to advance.

At least for me, I find much more peace when creating and functioning from a position of rest, peace, and contentment instead of constantly striving for more or better things just for the sake of getting more and better things.

GREAT THINGS ARE NOT DONE BY IMPULSE, BUT BY A SERIES OF SMALL THINGS BROUGHT TOGETHER.

- Vincent van Gogh -

CHAPTER 16: SOME CAUTIONS & CONCLUDING OBSERVATIONS

Many people will scoff at the idea that there is an exact science of getting rich. Believing that the supply of wealth is limited, they will insist that social and governmental institutions must be changed before any considerable number of people can acquire true wealth for themselves.

This is not true.

It is true that many existing governments keep the masses in poverty, but this is because the masses do not think currently think and act in a certain way. If the masses begin to move forward as suggested in this book, neither governments nor industrial systems could stop them. **All systems would need to be modified to accommodate the forward movement of society.**

If the people have the advancing mind, the faith that they can become rich, and move forward with the fixed purpose to become rich, nothing can possibly keep them in poverty.

Individuals may enter upon the certain way at any time under any government and make themselves rich. When any considerable number of individuals do so under any government, they will cause the system to be modified in a way that opens the way for others.

The more people who get rich on the competitive plane, the worse for others. The more who get rich on the creative plane, the better for others.

The economic liberation of the masses can only be accomplished by getting a large number of people to practice the creative and scientific method set down in this book to become rich. These will show others the way and inspire them with a desire for real life with the faith that it can be attained and with the purpose to attain it.

For the present, however, it is enough to know that neither the government under which you live nor the capitalistic or competitive system of industry can keep you from getting rich.

When you enter upon the creative plane of thought, you rise above all these things and become a citizen of another kingdom.

Remember that your thought must be held upon the creative plane. You are never for an instant to be betrayed into regarding the supply as limited or into acting on the level of competition.

Whenever you do fall into old ways of thought, correct yourself instantly.

When you are in the competitive mind, you have lost the cooperation of the mind of the infinite.

Do not spend any time in planning as to how you will meet possible emergencies in the future, except as things may affect your actions today. You should only be concerned with doing today's work in a perfectly successful and efficient manner, and not with emergencies which may arise tomorrow.

You can attend to them as they come.

Do not concern yourself with questions as to how you shall surmount obstacles which may loom upon your business horizon, unless you can see plainly that your course must be altered today in order to avoid them.

No matter how tremendous an obstruction may appear at a distance, you will often find that if you go on in the certain way it will disappear as you approach it - or that a way over, through, or around it will appear.

No possible combination of circumstances can defeat a man or woman who is proceeding to get rich along strictly scientific and creative lines. No man or woman who does this can fail to get rich any more than one can multiply two by two and fail to get four.

Give no anxious thought to possible disasters, obstacles, panics, or unfavorable combinations of circumstances.

There is time enough to meet such things if and when they present themselves before you in the immediate moment, and you will find that every difficulty carries with it the wherewithal for its overcoming.

RJR: *Given the nature of so much of our mass-media these days, this can be a very, very difficult thing to do. It can seem like everywhere we look there is drama, violence, fear, war, corruption, and that the world is falling apart.*

This is not true. *Statistically speaking, people the world over are living longer, healthier, and are better educated than ever before in human history. You would not know this if you get most of your information from the corporate news media on the right OR the left of the political aisle. I never went into journalism because the mantra has been for ages, "if it bleeds, it leads." Again, it doesn't have to be this way.*

That is not the type of worldview that is worth spreading or continuing to adhere to if you want to see things change for the better. *Focus your attention on what you can do, what you can create, and who you can connect with right where you are. Don't waste your precious energy and time giving yourself over to fear. Those who spread it are profiting from it at your expense. How does that make you feel?*

If you are passionate about making a positive difference in the world, good! Get involved in your local community. Volunteer to help out at a non-profit. Create art that inspires those who see it. Build something.

*As has been discussed repeatedly throughout this book - **USE YOUR CREATIVE ENERGY AS A FORCE FOR GOOD.** The money will come.*

Guard your speech. Never speak of yourself, your affairs, or of anything else in a discouraged or discouraging way.

Never admit the possibility of failure, or speak in a way that infers failure as a possibility. Never speak of the times as being hard, or of business conditions as being doubtful. Times may be hard and business doubtful for those who are on the competitive plane, but they can never be so for you.

You can create what you want, and you are above fear.

When others are having hard times and poor business, you will often find your greatest opportunities because you have trained yourself to see them.

Train yourself to think of and to look upon the world as a something which is becoming, which is growing; and to regard seeming evil as being only that which is undeveloped.

Always speak in terms of advancement. To do otherwise is to deny your faith and to deny your faith is to lose it.

Never allow yourself to stay stuck feeling disappointed. You may expect to have a certain thing at a certain time and not get it at that time and this will appear to you like failure.

If you hold to your faith and keep moving forward, you will find that the failure was only apparent.

RJR: *There have been many, many, many periods of extreme hardship and feelings of soul-crushing disappointment in the course of my career thus far. For each one, however, I can look back and point to something that happened some time after that led to a better situation than I would have experienced had I stayed where I was.*

There are so many questions that I have about the nature of our universe and the way the world works. There's one thing I know for sure, and that is that it does not serve anyone to stay stuck in their depressed perspective, constantly wallowing in regrets of their past, worries about the future, or complaining about their perceived lack of opportunities. It simply is not useful.

As Wattles says throughout this book, when you shift your focus from what you don't have to what you do have and pay more attention to what you can do, right here and right now...things start changing for you. As far as I can tell and understand it, that is "the certain way" that Wattles talks about.

Go on in the certain way, and if you do not receive that thing, you will receive something so much better that you will see the seeming failure was really a great success.

A student of this science had set his mind on making a certain business deal which seemed to him at the time to be very desirable, and he worked for some weeks to bring it about. When the crucial time came, the thing failed in a perfectly inexplicable way. It was as if some unseen influence had been working secretly against him.

He was not disappointed. On the contrary, he thanked God that his desire had been overruled, and went steadily on with a grateful mind. In a few weeks an opportunity so much better came his way that he would not have made if he had taken the first deal. He saw that something which knew more than he knew had prevented him from losing the greater good by entangling himself with the lesser.

That is the way every seeming failure will work out for you if you keep your faith, hold to your purpose, have gratitude, and do every day all that can be done that day, doing each separate act in a successful and efficient manner. When you make a failure, it is because you have not asked for enough.

Keep on and a larger thing than you were seeking will certainly come to you. Remember this.

You will not fail because you lack the necessary talent to do what you wish to do. If you go on as I have directed, you will develop all the talent that is necessary to the doing of your work.

It is not within the scope of this book to deal with the science of cultivating talent, but it is as certain and simple as the process of getting rich.

RJR: *As it pertains to "talent", my opinion on this matter is simple: talent is something that is developed and practiced rigorously over time. There are certainly a small select few individuals who seem to have a natural propensity for whatever their skillset is, but a curious thing appears when you study the behavior of those individuals. They all practice their craft with focused intention and spend what most would consider inordinate and obsessive amounts of time getting better at what they do.*

In a nutshell, dear reader, the development of talent and riches all boils down to a few things: focus, self-discipline, work, practice, and learning to roll with the punches of life instead of letting them keep you down.

If you know this going into any endeavor, it becomes much easier to deal with the inevitable setbacks that you will encounter along the way.

Remember why you got started in the first place and keep the course. Success is a journey, not a destination.

Do not hesitate or waver in fear that when you come to any certain place that you will fail for lack of ability.

Keep right on and when you come to that place, the ability will be there for you.

The same source of ability which enabled the untaught Lincoln to do the greatest work in government ever accomplished by a single man is open to you.

You may draw upon the infinite intelligence that is there for wisdom to use in meeting the responsibilities which are laid upon you. Go on in full faith.

Study this book. Make it your constant companion until you have mastered all the ideas contained in it. While you are getting firmly established in this, you will do well to give up most recreations and pleasure and to stay away from places where conflicting ideas are shared in lectures or sermons.

Do not read pessimistic or conflicting literature or get into arguments about the matter. Spend most of your leisure time in contemplating your vision, cultivating gratitude, and in reading this book.

It contains all you need to know of the science of getting rich.

You will find all the essentials summed up in the following chapter.

RJR: *As it pertains to 'giving up most recreations and pleasure', I would not go that far. It is scientific fact that people are healthier when they are playing more and enjoying regular recreation time. (For more on this, read "Play" by Stuart Brown and Christopher Vaughan and "Rest" by Alex Soojung-Kim Pang.)*

I think if Wattles were around today, what he would likely say is more along the lines of "don't waste your life binging in front of the television/ computer/phone or frittering your time away just browsing social media, the internet, or playing video games."

As mentioned elsewhere - what this really boils down to is that people who "get rich" and are "successful" are usually those who spend a lot more time and energy working on bringing their dreams and their ideas to life than the average person.

That might not be something that those who are looking for a shortcut want to hear - but it is the truth.

You have it within you to accomplish whatever you put your mind to.

The question is...what are you going to DO about it?

OUR DEEPEST FEAR IS NOT THAT WE ARE INADEQUATE. OUR DEEPEST FEAR IS THAT WE ARE POWERFUL BEYOND MEASURE. IT IS OUR LIGHT, NOT OUR DARKNESS THAT MOST FRIGHTENS US.

WE ASK OURSELVES, "WHO AM I TO BE BRILLIANT, GORGEOUS, TALENTED, & FABULOUS?"

ACTUALLY, WHO ARE YOU NOT TO BE? YOU ARE A CHILD OF GOD. YOUR PLAYING SMALL DOES NOT SERVE THE WORLD.

THERE IS NOTHING ENLIGHTENED ABOUT SHRINKING SO THAT OTHER PEOPLE WON'T FEEL INSECURE AROUND YOU.

WE WERE BORN TO MAKE MANIFEST THE GLORY OF GOD THAT IS WITHIN US. IT'S NOT JUST IN SOME OF US.

IT'S IN EVERYONE. AS WE LET OUR OWN LIGHT SHINE, WE UNCONSCIOUSLY GIVE OTHER PEOPLE PERMISSION TO DO THE SAME. AS WE ARE LIBERATED FROM OUR OWN FEAR, OUR PRESENCE AUTOMATICALLY LIBERATES OTHERS.

- Marianne Williamson -

CHAPTER 17: A SUMMARY OF THE SCIENCE OF GETTING RICH

- **There is a thinking stuff from which all things are made.** In its original state, permeates, penetrates, and fills the interspaces of the universe.

- **A thought in this substance produces the thing that is imagined by the thought.**

- **Humanity can form things in their thoughts.** By impressing their thoughts/imagination upon formless substance *(paper, clay, musical scales, white boards...any kind of blank canvas)*, they can cause the things they think about to be created.

- **In order to do this, humanity must pass from the competitive to the creative mind.** Otherwise, they cannot be in harmony with the formless intelligence, which is always creative and never competitive in spirit.

- **Humanity may come into full harmony with the formless substance by entertaining a lively and sincere gratitude for the blessings it bestows upon them.** Gratitude unifies the mind of humanity with the intelligence of the formless substance.

- **Humanity can remain upon the creative plane only by uniting themselves with the formless intelligence through a deep and continuous feeling of gratitude.**

- **You must form a clear mental picture of the things you want.** Do with faith and purpose all that can be done each day to achieve that goal, doing each separate thing in an efficient manner.

- **You must hold this mental image in your thoughts, while being deeply grateful that all your desires are being granted to you.** The person who wishes to get rich must spend their leisure hours in contemplating their vision and in earnest thanksgiving that the reality is being given to them.

- **Too much stress cannot be laid on the importance of frequent contemplation of your mental image, coupled with unwavering faith and devout gratitude.** This is the process by which the creative forces are set in motion.

- **You must act NOW upon the people and things in your present environment.** The creative energy works through the established channels of natural growth and through the industrial and social order. What you want will come to you through the ways of established trade and commerce.

- **In order to receive your own when it comes, you must be active and this activity can only consist in more than filling your present place.** You must keep in mind the purpose to get rich through the realization of your mental image/vision.

- **You must give to everyone a use value that is greater than the cash value you receive, so that each transaction makes for more life and benefit of those you work with.** You must so hold the advancing thought that the impression of increase will be communicated to all with whom you come in contact.

Those who practice the foregoing instructions will certainly get rich.

The riches they receive will be in exact proportion to the definiteness of their vision, the fixity of their purpose, the steadiness of their faith, and the depth of their gratitude.

IF YOU CAN'T FEED A HUNDRED PEOPLE, THEN FEED JUST ONE.

- Mother Theresa -

AFTERWORD BY RYAN J. RHOADES

So now what? Well, it boils down to this: don't just sit around and wait for something to happen - go get started!

Work at your goals every day. Write them down somewhere that you can see them regularly. Make a vision board. Surround yourself with people of like-mind who are pursuing similar goals. Avoid hanging around negative and pessimistic people. They will only drag you down.

I obviously cannot make any specific claims as to how much money you will make, as every person is different and every situation varies based on a wide array of factors.

However, what I can say is that everyone has all kinds of great ideas that can lead to creating an amazing life for themselves that is far more exciting than just taking orders all day sitting in a cubicle.

Yes, that means you can too! *(If you put in the work to make it happen, of course.)*

The overall gist of this book is simply the following:

If you learn to lean into and harness your own creativity, you can monetize your ideas, start your own business endeavors, and CREATE wealth for yourself and your loved ones instead of always looking to earn it from an employer.

Some of the wealthiest people in the world arrived at their position through bringing their own creative ideas to life. It takes time. It takes practice. It takes patience. But it works. And it's worth it. **If you commit to building something of value, you can (and should) learn how to profit from it.**

So why wait?

Do what you can, with what you have, where you are.

I have included additional resources at the end of the book that may help you further in your quest for success. You never know what opportunities are waiting for you right around the corner.

More than anything, thanks for joining me on this journey and picking up this book. I came across the original a number of years ago in a thrift shop when I was struggling very intensely with my own financial troubles and I deeply understand what it is like to not know where your next rent check is coming from.

Things have definitely improved for me and my family since then, and I know that a number of the lessons that I took from Wallace Wattles' suggestions have made a big difference in my quality of life and the way I view the world around me. You may not agree with all of it - much the same way that I didn't - but as with anything in life, it's best to test things out and see what works for you.

If you have any questions, comments, or want some help bringing your own ideas to life, feel free to reach out to me at my website which can be found at http://www.ReformDesigns.biz or connect with me on social media.

I wish you much joy, peace, abundance, more wealth than you know what to do with, and the wisdom to use it all for good. More than that, may you find your voice, happiness, love, and contentment in the process.

You can do this. Now go get started!

- Ryan J. Rhoades,
Salem OR - July, 2018

FAITH IS TAKING THE FIRST STEP EVEN WHEN YOU DON'T SEE THE WHOLE STAIRCASE.

- Martin Luther King, Jr. -

RECOMMENDED READING

"Great leaders create opportunities that equip and mobilize others... and they don't just grow leaders, they multiply them."
- Steve Addison

"In a time of drastic change, it is the learners who inherit the future. The learned find themselves equipped to live in a world that no longer exists."
- Eric Hoffer

Over the years, I have found that it is much easier to take the advice of those who have gone before me than to constantly be trying to reinvent the wheel. In school, reading books was often a horrible, agitating chore that we had to do in order to pass a test or write a paper. You've got to get over that mentality if you want to really take your life and your business endeavors to the next level.

Some of the wealthiest and most well educated people in the world have taken the time to invest in anyone who is willing to listen by writing books. Oftentimes they are available for free at your local library or for less than $20 apiece online or in a local book store.

You can only learn so much from the seemingly endless supply of click bait "listicles" these days, and your information retention level *(that is, how much of what you read that you remember)* will be much higher if you don't have obnoxious advertisements interrupting your train of thought while you're trying to learn something new.

The books listed here are all books I have benefited from personally in one way or another. You will find that much of this creative journey is about cultivating mindset and practice, not tools.

You will also most likely find that trying to keep up with the monstrosity of what social and corporate media has become is not only a huge waste of time, money, and energy - but also that your emotional, mental, and oftentimes physical health will improve dramatically when you don't spend so much time consuming it.

Over the years, our best clients and experiences have come from cultivating closer relationships with the people who are already listening as opposed to trying to reach the masses or "go viral". That stuff is so overrated, unfulfilling, and not sustainable.

Do what you love and what leaves the world at least a little bit better than you found it. Work with people who are doing what you believe in. Learn from those who you look up to. Ask lots of questions. Most people are often more willing to share the lessons they've learned along the way than people realize.

Chances are high you won't get to the end of your life wishing you had worked more.

You will wish you had been more intentional about what you did with your life and with whom. So why not start now?

Don't stress out so much about all the things you can't do - focus on what you can where you're at, keep practicing, and be intentional about educating yourself.

Most of "real life" isn't like school - there's nobody telling you what books to read - you get to choose! My advice is simply this: pursue and learn about things that you enjoy and do what you can to figure out how to monetize those passions.

You have literally nothing to lose and everything to gain.

Thanks for reading - make sure to go to https://www.ScienceOfGettingRich.info for direct links to all of the books mentioned here (and more!)

RECOMMENDED READING

Stop Wasting Time & Burning Money
by Ryan J. Rhoades & Lany Sullivan

The Soul of Money
by Lynn Twist

The E-Myth Revisited
by Michael Gerber

Think and Grow Rich
by Napoleon Hill

The War of Art, Turning Pro, and *The Artist's Journey*
by Steven Pressfield

Rework
by Jason Fried & David Heinemeier Hansson

How to Think Like Leonardo da Vinci
by Michael J. Gelb

The Artist's Way
by Julia Cameron

How to Win Friends and Influence People
by Dale Carnegie

The 7 Habits of Highly Effective People
by Steven Covey

Damn Good Advice
by George Lois

RECOMMENDED READING

Books by Tim Ferriss:

Tools of Titans
Tribe of Mentors
The Four Hour Workweek
The Four Hour Chef
The Four Hour Body

Books by Seth Godin:

The Dip
Tribes
Purple Cow
Linchpin

Books by James Altucher:

Choose Yourself
Reinvent Yourself
The Power of No

Books by Austin Kleon:

Steal Like an Artist
Show Your Work

Books by Ryan Holiday:

The Obstacle is the Way
Perennial Seller
Trust Me, I'm Lying: Confessions of a Media Manipulator
(this one is excellent to better understand how 'media' works)

RECOMMENDED READING

Books by Kamal Ravikant:

Love Yourself Like Your Life Depends On It
Rebirth

Books by Michael Michalko:

Thinkertoys
Creative Thinkering

Books by John Warrillow:

Built to Sell
The Automatic Customer

Books by Brendon Burchard:

The Millionaire Messenger
The Charge
Life's Golden Ticket
High Performance Habits
The Motivation Manifesto

Start With Why
by Simon Sinek

Guerrilla Marketing
by Jay Conrad Levinson

Ogilvy on Advertising
by David Ogilvy

RECOMMENDED READING

Delivering Happiness
by Tony Hsieh

Brainshare
by Joe Siecinski

The Alchemist
by Paulo Coelho

Fahrenheit 451
by Ray Bradbury

1984
by George Orwell

The Hunger Games Trilogy
by Suzanne Collins

Ready Player One
by Ernest Cline

The Hobbit and Lord of the Rings Trilogy
by J.R.R. Tolkien

The Time Keeper and *Tuesdays with Morrie*
by Mitch Albom

The Noticer and *The Noticer Returns*
by Andy Andrews

Ishmael
by Daniel Quinn

RECOMMENDED READING

Strengths Finder 2.0
by Tom Rath

Mastery
by Robert Greene

Rising Strong
by Brené Brown

Big Magic
by Elizabeth Gilbert

The Success Principles
by Jack Canfield

*The Suble Art of Not Giving a F*ck*
by Mark Manson

The Magic of Thinking Big
by David J. Schwartz, PhD

Mindfulness for Beginners
by Jon Kabat-Zinn

The Last Lecture
by Randy Pausch

Developing the Leader Within You
by John C. Maxwell

Don't Worry, Make Money and *Don't Sweat the Small Stuff*
by Richard Carlson

RECOMMENDED READING

The Hero with a Thousand Faces
by Joseph Campbell

The Writer's Journey
by Christopher Vogler

The World as I See It and *Out of My Later Years*
by Albert Einstein

Mastery
by George Leonard

The Richest Man Who Ever Lived
by Steven K. Scott

The Power of Patience
by M.J. Ryan

Awareness
by Anthony de Mello

Ignore Everybody and 39 Other Keys to Creativity
by Hugh MacLeod

This is Your Brain on Music
by Daniel J. Levitin

Unlimited Power
by Tony Robbins

Profit First
by Mike Michalowicz

RECOMMENDED READING

The Leader Phrase Book
by Patrick Alain

The Law of Success
by Napoleon Hill

The Power of Full Engagement
by Jim Loehr and Tony Schwartz

Blue Ocean Strategy and *Blue Ocean Shift*
by W. Chan Kim and Renée A. Mauborgne

The Lean Startup
by Eric Ries

Striking Thoughts
by Bruce Lee

The Life Changing Magic of Tidying Up
by Marie Kondo

The Art of Peace
by Morihei Ueshiba and John Stevens

Play It Away: A Workaholic's Cure for Anxiety
by Charlie Hoehn

Book Yourself Solid
Michael Port

*The Starfish and the Spider:
The Unstoppable Power of Leaderless Organizations*
by Ori Brafman & Rod Beckstrom

ADDITIONAL RESOURCES

Your Local Small Business Development Center (https://www.sba.gov/tools/local-assistance/sbdc)

Chances are high that you have a local Small Business Development Center near you. The SBDC gives free business advice and mentoring to pretty much anyone that wants it. Our local SBDC has been very instrumental in helping us learn the art and nuances of running our own business endeavors as well as working together to get us better connected in our community.

StartupStash.com

This is a great site that is full of more resources than you will know what to do with - but the nice thing is that it is extremely well organized by a wide variety of topics. Stuff like marketing, design, software to use for pretty much anything you can think of, generating ideas, web hosting, etc.

1000 True Fans by Kevin Kelly (http://kk.org/thetechnium/1000-true-fans/)

This article is a quintessential read for anyone who wants to do anything "creative" for a living. You can also find videos on YouTube on the topic.

"A true fan is defined as a fan that will buy anything you produce," Kelly says - and in the article he talks about how to go about forming an action plan for reaching those true fans and building a following, a product, and a business around it.

ADDITIONAL RESOURCES

Khan Academy
(https://www.khanacademy.org)

The Khan Academy was founded by educator Salman Khan in 2006 as a non-profit educational organization dedicated to providing online tutoring and learning services to users across a wide variety of topics. I can't recommend this site highly enough if you are wanting to learn just about anything.

Masterclass.com

Want to learn how to compose music with Hans Zimmer? Maybe you want to learn how to shoot hoops with Stephen Curry? Or perhaps you'd like to learn all about acting from Helen Mirren? Whatever topic you are interested in, chances are you can learn a lot from the masters at Masterclass.com. This is a paid subscription service but I have found it to be well, well worth the investment.

Makerbook.net

This is a nicely organized directory of resources for "creative types" and anyone who is working on building their own thing. Photography, product mockups, graphics, textures, fonts, audio and more. Enjoy!

NOTES & PERSONAL THOUGHTS

NOTES & PERSONAL THOUGHTS

NOTES & PERSONAL THOUGHTS

NOTES & PERSONAL THOUGHTS

NOTES & PERSONAL THOUGHTS

NOTES & PERSONAL THOUGHTS

NOTES & PERSONAL THOUGHTS

NOTES & PERSONAL THOUGHTS

THANK YOU's

This book would not exist without the encouragement and support of more people than I can fit here, but there are a few that I want to mention specifically.

First of all, to my wife - thank you for your continued love and companionship over the years as we have traveled this creative journey together. The best is yet to come and I would not be who I am without you. You truly are my best friend and I love you beyond words.

To my parents and my sisters - thank you for always encouraging me to pursue my dreams, even when the road has been difficult at times. I love and appreciate you and look forward to seeing you soon.

To Brent and Daniel - thank you for your listening ear, your hopeful words, your strength, and your vision. You have believed in me when many others have doubted, and I cannot thank you enough for being such great and supportive friends.

To Sarah - thanks for your help with editing this manuscript and the relentless motivation you have shared with us over the years to keep moving forward. It's been a wild ride, but I'm glad we're all in this together.

To the rest of our brilliant creator friends, family, mentors, advisers, and fans - thank you. We love you. You are the reason we create. We believe in you and so appreciate all of your help and support over the years. Now go forth and make something amazing!

reformation
➤➤DESIGNS

Thanks so much for reading!

Do you need help bringing your own creative ideas to life?

Contact us today for a free consultation!

www.ReformDesigns.biz

the reformation DESIGNS store

Looking for some stylish new swag, gifts, or wall decor?

Go to www.RDShop.biz today and check out our online store!

**Make sure to visit
www.ScienceOfGettingRich.info
for recommended reading,
resources, merch, and more!**